CHILDREN OF POVERTY

STUDIES ON THE EFFECTS
OF SINGLE PARENTHOOD,
THE FEMINIZATION OF POVERTY,
AND HOMELESSNESS

edited by

STUART BRUCHEY
UNIVERSITY OF MAINE

A GARLAND SERIES

YOUTH IN FOSTER CARE

THE SHORTCOMINGS OF CHILD PROTECTION SERVICES

BONITA EVANS

GARLAND PUBLISHING, INC.
NEW YORK & LONDON / 1997

Library of Congress Cataloging-in-Publication Data

Evans, Bonita, 1940–
  Youth in foster care : the shortcomings of child protection
services / Bonita Evans.
    p.   cm. — (Children of poverty)
  Includes bibliographical references and index.
  ISBN 0-8153-3020-0 (alk. paper)
  1. Foster children—United States. 2. City children—United
States. 3. Minorities—United States. 4. Foster home care—United
States. 5. Neighborhood—United States. 6. Assimilation (Sociol-
ogy) I. Title. II. Series.
HV881.E9 1997
362.73'3'0973—dc21   97-36983

Printed on acid-free, 250-year-life paper
Manufactured in the United States of America

In Loving Memory of
Verna Ashton Evans, a mother for whom
No sacrifice was too great.

Contents

Tables

Figures

Acknowledgments

In Appreciation of

Professors A.L. Giusti, G.A. Gustafson, and B. Persky,
without whom this task would have been impossible to accomplish.

List of Abbreviations

ACLUF. American Civil Liberties Union Foundation.

AFCARS. Adoption and Foster Care Analysis Reporting System.

APD. Antisocial Personality Disorder. A serious mental disorder experienced by individuals over the age of 18, which is traceable to the earlier condition, conduct disorder. The individual lacks affection, respect for others, and society in general; is egocentric, manipulative, can be homicidal and cannot be trusted. (See American Psychiatric Association's Diagnostic and Statistical Manual IV under same heading [1994]).

CD. Conduct Disorder. A predecessor to the more serious mental condition of antisocial personality disorder. Is most often seen in younger people who have a potential for it to stabilize into APD in adulthood. (See American Psychiatric Association's Diagnostic and Statistical Manual IV under same heading [1994]).

CDR. Children's Defense Fund.

C & Y (Department of Children & Youth). Local child welfare department reporting to the DHS and DPS.

DHS. Department of Human Services.

DPW. Department of Public Welfare.

FCDA. Foster Care Data Archive.

GED. General Equivalency Diploma. Granted on satisfactory completion of an examination of subjects at 12th grade level and is the equivalent of a high school diploma.

IEP. Individualized Educational Planning.

MP. Multiple Personalities. A mental disorder in which the individual actually lives out and experiences his/herself as other people.

Youth in Foster Care

I

Introduction

A society's civilization is measured, humanity tested and future shaped by how it protects and cares for its children. (*Christian Children's Fund, 1994*).

Over the past two decades those youths whose lifestyles are either consciously, or involuntarily affected by the threat of violence, or the prospect of negative outcome, have been defined as being "at risk." Being at risk may take the form of a dysfunctional family, coercion through peer group pressure, inferior education, poor housing, or physical health, due to malnutrition. Malnutrition often expresses itself in a failure to learn and in some cases, is misdiagnosed. The student is then categorized as having a learning disability. Students suffering from malnutrition are often unable to retain information in their short-term memory, and exhibit symptoms similar to those who have intellectual problems.

At risk, as it pertains to behavior, covers a wide spectrum of activity, including drug peddling, gang membership, unprotected sex, thrill seeking, and psychological states which have been categorized by the *Diagnostic and Statistical Manual of Mental Disorders IV* (DSM) as psychopathy.

This study examined several factors, which exacerbate the potential for increased violence and psychopathy in young people who become wards of the state, using both observation and the researcher's experiences as a teacher working with youths (aged 6-21) in emotional

3

support classes. Additionally, the researcher was able to work for a while as a counselor in a group home environment.

The two case studies cited in this work are taken from the researcher's written accounts of group home residents. Two reflective cases have also been taken from the Baby Neal Civil Action, conducted by the American Civil Liberties Union Foundation (ACLUF), and are included, as support for the researcher's contention that the child protective services system is failing. The repercussions of this failure can be identified in the classroom and the foster care environment, regardless of where in the United States youth are being fostered.

THE PURPOSE OF THE STUDY

The Purpose of the study was to determine the impact of systemic shortcomings on the domestic and educational conditions of youth in the foster care system. In addition to studying the impact of systemic failures on foster care arrangements, the study also examined the impact of the protection services' failure to work more closely with youth, and with teachers on student educational outcomes. The researcher sought to discover data which would provide answers to the following questions:

1. How do present foster care arrangements contribute to social disaffection in minority children in care?
2. What role does contextual environment play in shaping the realities of minority adolescents?
3. How does the lack of agency/foster parent liaison portend negative outcomes for youth in care.

It is hoped that this review of the shortcomings of the foster care system and their impact on both the social and educational environments of youth in care will become a catalyst for a more in-depth study in both areas. In approaching the task, the goal was to become more conversant with the physical and mental conditions of minority inner-city youths being fostered in rural areas.

DESIGN OF THE STUDY

The study was a causal research study which employed observation, case studies, interviews, questionnaires, and resource materials (annual reports, journals, agency newsletters and broadcast interviews) to determine conditions which affect both the efficient functioning of the child protective services and the welfare of youth in its care. Two subjects were observed, a female and a male. Data pertaining to the female was drawn from the researcher's written accounts of the girl's experiences in the group home. As regards the male, he was known to the researcher for a period of not less than six months, both as a student and as a group home resident.

The researcher also had an opportunity to talk with the male subject about his concerns in connection with the living arrangements at both his foster home and the group home. Prior to his arrival at the group home, the researcher spoke with his special education teacher and also his foster parents in casual conversation, which revealed some of the facts cited in the case study. However, the majority of the information compiled in respect of this case was the result of the researcher's observations and interactions with him at school, as his teacher, and on various occasions.

INSTRUMENTATION AND PROCEDURE

The researcher employed both observation and conversation in compiling information on the two youths examined in her personal case studies. Observations were carried out on a weekly and sometimes daily basis, as in the case of Marlene, the female subject. The detailed observations of this particular case were incorporated into the study with a view to providing the reader with a psychological profile of a client who experienced gradual mental deterioration over the period of her stay in care.

With a view to supporting the researcher's contention that the conditions experienced by the two youths were not isolated incidents in terms of out-of-home care, the researcher selected two reflective case studies under investigation by the ACLUF. The first case was that of a young female, Sherry G. It provided information regarding events which eventually led to the psychological deterioration of the client, and revealed that the agency took little care in effecting any form of program to prevent this condition. The second was that of John B., a 14-year-old, whom the agency left to his own devices on a number of occasions. The two reflective cases have been incorporated into the study with a view to illustrating agency negligence with respect to adolescent clients, regardless of whether the client is in care or truant.

Through the exploration of the four cases, the reader is given some insight into many organizational factors which affect the provision of effective and efficient service to youth in care. Additional to the incorporation of the two reflective studies, the researcher also employed three methods of data collection, professional journals and field-related studies, observation, interviews, and questionnaires.

Data was derived from observations made over a two-year period, in combination with practical experience in the special education classrooms and in group homes. This was carried out by the researcher with a view to determining the impact of the systemic shortcomings in organizational policy and practice on clients in group home care and in the classroom.

The area investigated was one which is closed, so it was necessary to hire a college senior in social sciences from the local college as a research assistant to present the questionnaires. This was necessary because teachers/educators would only respond to questionnaires presented by members of the local population. The researcher instructed the research assistant as to the information she was to obtain and the manner in which the questionnaire was to be presented. This was done to protect the identities of the teachers so that they would not receive negative feedback from the agency or the school administration.

The questionnaires were responded to anonymously and did not require that the teachers' names, or any information which would identify them, be provided. Teachers from elementary, middle, and high school were provided with the questionnaire. The researcher received nine responses from the number selected, using a survey population of approximately 12-18 teachers selected from different schools. The responses comprised three teachers working at 1st-3rd grade level, three at 5th-8th, and three at 9th-12th.

The researcher decided that it would also be informative to circulate the same questionnaire to mainstream teachers, as there is a new policy that some special education students should be mainstreamed, if possible, behavior and academic performance, permitting. (See questionnaire at Annex D)

DATA COLLECTION AND OTHER PROCEDURES

1. Through the use of secondary sources, the researcher determined the number of children in out-of-home care on a nationwide basis.
2. Employing journals, magazines, news items, educational television programs, personal observations, questionnaires, and annual reports, the researcher determined the systemic problems associated with the foster care system.
3. Professional journals, studies, public broadcasts, interviews, and questionnaires were used to determine existing problems, and how they impact youth in care.
4. The information received from secondary sources was compared with the researcher's experiences and observations in both the classroom and in the group home environments.
5. By employing the interview method with accompanying questionnaire as a control measure, the researcher discovered what problems foster parents encounter when they agree to take foster children, which are due to systemic problems related to information, follow-up service, and finance.
6. The researcher collected annual reports and other information circulated for public information and to potential foster parents.
7. The researcher conducted a random survey of special education teachers at elementary, middle and high school level, using questionnaires to determine any systemic problems of the child protective services which negatively

impact on their efforts to educate foster/group home students in the classroom.

SCOPE AND LIMITATIONS

The research for this project was designed to focus mainly on the rural area of northeastern Pennsylvania. Due to the paucity of foster parents, the study was limited in the number of foster parents who were interviewed. There were only 7 minority foster parents on the roles of the Department of Children and Youth. Of these, the researcher selected three (representing nearly 50% of the available African-American foster parents. The number of African-American families available for interview, in itself, indicates systemic biases in the system, and is discussed in more detail later.

Fortunately, each of the foster families interviewed had worked with at least three agencies. The youths taken into their care ranged in age from 0-17 years. This wide range of experience proved extremely helpful in obtaining information both as to the difficulties posed by the paucity of agency/client relations and the lack of historical resources available to each client on the child in care. Most parents worked with the same agencies, but at different periods. They also fostered youths who had various problems. This provided an opportunity for the researcher to see how the same and different agencies reacted to foster parents in varying circumstances.

With respect to the survey of special and mainstream teachers taken during the course of the research, the researcher was not content that the findings would prove the pervasiveness of systemic shortcomings and their impact on foster youth in classrooms. The questionnaire was circulated at a teachers' conference held in Florida by a doctoral student, who assisted the researcher by selecting 20 additional teachers from different states in the categories previously mentioned. The researcher then compared these responses to those of the Pennsylvania teachers. The questionnaire was then circulated to several New Jersey teachers and teachers in New York. The responses to the questions provided in the questionnaire were practically identical.

II

The Problem

A major factor contributing to the troubling environment which foster youths create when they are removed to new areas, is the frequency with which these changes occur, and often, the rapidity. In many cases, foster children find that just when they are settling in and beginning to trust and develop a relationship with the foster family, they are moved. The most common reason for the change is the behavior of the ward, but in some cases it is the health of the foster parent, which prompts the change. In many instances, no record is kept of the number of reassignments made by the child. A paucity of familial history on the child in combination with multiple placements, makes it difficult for potential foster parents to discern the adaptability and psychological stability of the child.

The child protective services systems have failed to meet the needs of youth in care, due to ineffective methods of storing data related to placement outcome. The paucity of foster and adoptive homes, in combination with the lack of staff, and the selection of poorly qualified staff, or staff whose attitudes are not appropriate to the task have also taken a toll on agency effectiveness. The consequent condition is lack of follow up on the outcomes of youth in care. Youth with serious emotional and health problems are left untreated, or receive treatment which is fragmented due to; (a) the reluctance of practitioners to service patients on Medicaid, and (b) the number of placements each youth has before leaving care. Multiple placements result in breaks in the continuity of health care by the physicians and psychologists.

In group homes and in special education classes, psychologically stable youths often reside, or study with youths who are unstable, thus creating a potentially dangerous and violent environment for both types of youth. As well, students are often misdiagnosed because of their behavior. The behavior perceived as maladaptive, might, over a longer period of time, be found to have its basis in a transient state of instability and diagnosed as a manifestation of the confusion the youth feels about events which have affected his/her life prior to arriving at the new location. In some cases the behavior is a reaction to a sense of alienation which is felt by adolescents at being suddenly imposed upon a different environment and having it imposed upon them. Often the living skills which helped these young people survive in the former environment, are inappropriate for the new. Behavior defined and regarded as "inappropriate," could also be a major factor contributing to alienation in student/teacher and client/therapist relationships. It is certainly an area which deserves further study.

With regard to the classroom environment, Healy's (1990) study of the children with learning disabilities—a significant factor contributing to inappropriate behavior—reveals that between 1976 and 1985, there was a 135% increase in the diagnosed cases of learning disability, representing a figure of 1,867,447, up from an earlier figure of 796,596. By 1988, nearly 15,000 children nationwide, per week were being assessed for learning disorders (139). Under the present methods used for assessing learning disorders, up to 80% of America's children could be diagnosed as learning disabled. It is impossible at this juncture to determine how much of this figure is attributable to efforts to employ assessment as a means of dispensing with troublesome students. In 1990, the number of students diagnosed as having attention deficit hyperactivity disorder (ADHD) was estimated at 1 million to 4.5 million, the majority of whom were boys (139).

In some classrooms more than 50% of the student body has been diagnosed as hyperactive. This situation has resulted in a related increase in the use of stimulant drugs to increase the span of the student's attention and manageability. It is estimated that 6% of

American school children are being given prescription drugs, (e.g., Ritalin) with a view to making them more manageable in class. Parents, to counteract drug rebound and enable the youths to behave properly at home, (139-140) often augment these daily dosages. Many doctors complain that the number of children treated with Ritalin is much higher than it should be. Some studies have shown that the level of dosage needed to make teachers approve of the student's behavior is so high, that it actually dulls reasoning ability (157). Questions to be raised by this finding relate not only to the type of work done in the classroom, but also to the real source of the problem. The largest number of referrals are made because the student appears to have problems related to understanding or expressing verbal material as well as reading, writing, and spelling. (See figure at Appendix A).

Hyperactivity is another facet of the learning disability question. Healy (1990) speaking of hyperactivity, refers to research conducted by Dr. Diane McGuiness as follows:

> Dr. McGuiness who confesses she is irate about the amount of Ritalin being prescribed today believes that many children thought to be "hyperactive" are really normally vigorous children, 'who refuse to abide by adult admonitions to sit still and conform to rules set by adults for their own convenience (157).

Sharing the same perception are Serwatka, Deering, and Grant (1995) who examined the factors which led to a disproportionately high representation of African-Americans in emotionally handicapped classes. Their findings revealed that in many instances their placement in these classes can be attributed to factors which are basic to racial difference. For example, the teacher, or psychologist may view the motoric precocity of African-American children as an indication of hyperactivity, which requires referral for assessment for an emotional handicap. Also, the findings revealed that due to the African-American students' affinity for intense stimuli, they tend to do less well in non-stimulating, monotonous environments, which is reflected in their reaction to the classroom environment. Lastly, the researchers stated that students from lower economic environments are more often victimized by crime in their neighborhoods than are other students, and this is a significant factor contributing to the adoption of similar patterns of behavior. In most cases, aggressive role play is used by the child as a protective means of coping with perceived external threat. This type of behavior is often misperceived as an indicator of emotional disturbance in the school setting (493).

BACKGROUND

Over the past 10 years, class action suits have been brought against 25 states, counties, and cities in the United States, in an effort to reform the child protection services (Simms & Halfon, 1994, 510). The foster care system as it presently exists is failing to meet the needs of children in care. The American Civil Liberties Union Foundation (ACLUF) has undertaken a class action suit on behalf of 6,000 children in care in Pennsylvania (the area studied in this paper). The ACLUF cites the defendants, the Commonwealth of Pennsylvania, and the city of Philadelphia as having violated the plaintiffs' federal, constitutional, and state statutory rights by failing to provide the plaintiff children with legally mandated services. It further claims that Philadelphia's foster care system, which also provides clients for the rural area discussed in this study, is marked by inadequate investigations of child abuse and neglect, and is unable to provide sufficient services for children and families. This condition is the result of poor planning, inadequate care, a scarcity of placement resources, and the failure to provide permanent homes for children (*Neal et al. vs. Robert Casey et al.*, 1992).

The Commonwealth of Pennsylvania is further cited in the Baby Neal Case as having received substantial funds to assist it in conforming with the stipulations cited in the Adoption Assistance and Child Welfare Act of 1980, and the Federal Child Abuse Prevention and Treatment Act, 1983. Under the stipulations cited therein, the child protective services are responsible for the welfare of the children in the system; and are obligated to seek and provide a means of keeping children together with their natural parents, or alternatively, for providing permanent homes for children with adoptive families. Additionally, all children in foster care are to have written case plans, which are to be developed within specified periods, so that appropriate services can be provided to the children, their parents, and foster parents. These case plans should be designed to address the needs of each child (Federal Adoption Assistance Act, 1980).

One of the major factors negatively impacting the Commonwealth of Pennsylvania's ability to carry out the prescribed tasks is poor record keeping. It is not alone in its incapacity to meet the demands of federal and state stipulations. Courtney and Collins (1994) found that in each state, separate databases are used to record facts about youth in care. Unfortunately, records in respect of the cumulative number of placements to foster care or group home residences of youth in the system during the period of their stay in care, are improperly maintained (Penzerro & Lein, 1995).

This in many instances is due to the practice of removing information relating to previous placements when the youth receives a new placement (Courtney & Collins, 1994, 360). The failure to maintain accurate records results in many negative outcomes, which affect both the child and his/her family. In 1978, before the prolific increase in out-of-home care, The Children's Defense Fund published a report, which stated that children were being lost in the system and could not be located (258). Both the number of children in care and agencies handling foster care have increased since then, exacerbating the problem. Data is also lacking on the return of youths to public care after unsuccessful adoption. This practice serves only to present an incomplete history of the youth and misinforms prospective foster parents about the adaptability of the child to different environments.

Courtney and Collins continue, stating that in most states, child welfare services often find it difficult to give and exact accounting of "which" monies were expended on "what" type of services, and for "whom." The statement should, however, be counterbalanced by stating that there is accountability, but it does not as yet meet the criteria demanded by federal and state legislatures, which are demanding more detailed evidence that child welfare services are achieving their espoused goals (361).

A study conducted by Simms and Halfon (1994) revealed that it is very rare to find a child welfare service functioning at federal, state, or local level which provides specific programs to address the health care needs of children. This situation results in poor crisis-oriented care. Only on very rare occasions is it possible to find foster care agencies capable of monitoring whether children in their care are receiving even basic health care. Despite the prevalence of complex mental, physical and educational problems (25% of the children in foster care are in need of psychological services (Fanshel, 1992), many children requiring state special services, do not receive them (Simms and Halfon, 507).

Goerge, Wulczyn, and Fanshel (1994) oppose Courtney and Collin's view, arguing that those who criticize the method of disseminating information about outcomes in the child welfare system are shortsighted. It is their contention that with the initiation of the new Adoption and Foster Care Analysis and Reporting System (AFCARS) and the Statewide Automated Child Welfare Information System (SACWIS), information will be substantially increased (526). They do, however, believe that the effectiveness of these systems could be given a significant boost by the input of data based on findings of longitudinal studies. These studies would assist in linking clinical findings to organizational structure in terms of creating effective programs for child welfare. However, Goerge et al. warn that such approaches are costly and might be adequately replaced by the improved use of administrative data. Information collected as part of the clerical process is deemed by both groups of researchers to be poor.

Under the stipulations cited in The Adoption Assistance and Child Welfare Act 1980 (96-272), all states must maintain child-tracking systems containing information on location and goals for each child in foster care. All states, according to Goerge et al. have implemented some version of this database. But, as can be observed from the study conducted by Courtney and Collins, the data is not readily accessible from a single source.

To counteract arguments of this nature, Goerge et al. offer as an example of efforts to provide a national database of child welfare records, the Foster Care Data Archive (FCDA). Unfortunately, the archive contains data derived from only 5 states (Illinois, Michigan, New York, California and Texas)—representing less than 10% of the nation's states (509). Thus, the preceding does less to convince, than to confirm the legitimacy of the Courtney and Collins findings—at least for the present.

How relevant is the Courtney and Collins argument in terms of what is occurring in the state of Pennsylvania? Complaints launched against the state in the Baby Neal case, by the ACLUF, fall within the following categories and appear to revolve around matters which though systemic in nature, encompass both the functioning of the system and the disbursement of information, as can be surmised from the following:

SYSTEMIC FAILURES—FAILURE TO PROTECT CHILDREN

Caseloads held by workers investigating the neglect and abuse of children are not immediately followed up. One of the major reasons for this, is the lack of police protection for social workers, who are often obliged to enter dangerous areas in order to investigate the living conditions of children. Additionally, transportation is inadequate. In many cases, too few cars are available to meet the transportation needs of workers. In some cases, the existing cars are in such a dangerous state of disrepair that they cannot be used. Those which are available for use, must be returned to the office by 5:00 p.m. so that the administrators can use them to drive home. Lastly, workers are hampered by the fact that there is no standardized formula for carrying out an investigation, which accurately interprets data used to assess and determine the degree to which the child is at risk. Often the social worker's decision as to whether a child should be placed in care or not, is based on the availability of placement resources, regardless of the risk to the child.

The availability of services which would enable children to remain at home and avoid foster care are virtually non-existent for many families. The Services to Children in their Own Home (SCOH) program is accessible only through the Department of Human Services (DHS), or private agencies. In the case of the private agencies, funding is contingent upon the willingness of the DHS to disburse such moneys to these agencies, and the capacity of the agency to accept additional caseloads. Social workers endeavoring to provide SCOH also lack comprehensive information as to the specific services provided by the private agencies. In order to keep up the appearance that DHS caseloads are within manageable parameters, social workers are often directed to close cases designated as "low risk," despite the social workers' contentions that certain families require these services (ACLUF, 1990, 47-51).

INAPPROPRIATE PLACEMENT AND LACK OF PROPER CARE

In the case of infants and young children needing foster care, appropriate placement, is an area in which the DHS has experienced a good deal of failure. Many infants remain in the hospital long after they have been assessed as medically ready for discharge. The DHS has as many as 40-60 boarder babies at the hospital awaiting placement, daily. Additionally, many children categorized as being at risk, who have been removed from their homes are obliged to spend the night in the Department's offices and bathrooms because no placement can be found for them. In some cases, social workers have taken the children home with them in order that they can have a place to sleep.

Teenagers for whom no placements are available are "streeted"— told by social workers to go back to the streets and fend for themselves until a placement can be made. Streeting an adolescent is like tolling the death knell. Bruce Ritter's history of Covenant House, entitled *Sometimes God Has a Kid's Face* (1988*)*, describes the probability of survival on the streets:

> Kids don't survive very long on the street—at least in a recognizably
> human way. The distortion of the personality, the erosion of character
> are swift and massive and almost always irreversible (1988, ii).

The failure to place youth in care is further exacerbated by the fact that there is no central placement database which can be used by the protection services. Each social worker must contact the private agencies, as well as the DHS foster care section, individually. This results in an effort to find a bed of any type, which in turn has the consequence of overcrowding facilities.

Often a child is placed with untrained foster parents who are unable to deal with the child's problems, which results in multiple placements. As long as the foster family or agency does not reject the youth, the Department will continue to keep the youth in that placement indefinitely. As a consequence, youths in the Department's foster homes often remain for long periods of time in a care situation which has not been thoroughly investigated.

Exacerbating the situation is the fact that the Department has no clear guidelines, or procedures for determining which youths should be placed with private agencies. The quality of care is not uniform in the private agencies and the Department has no effective method for determining whether the agencies are providing the minimal acceptable standards of care for clients (ACLUF, 1990, 51-56).

The lack of information on the service provided by child welfare organizations, in combination with little, or no information with respect to who is providing these services and under what conditions, has in rural Pennsylvania, led to a disintegration of the services provided and a racially biased system. Under the present system, African-American social workers, teachers, and those qualified to assist minority group home residents and students (the funding for which can be as high as $80,000 and the median $50,000 per child, per year [ACLUF, 1994]) are prevented from enjoying the security of employment-related benefits to be derived from working with this specific population. For example, the board of education of Monroe County, in the Pocono Mountain area of Pennsylvania, employs less than five African-American teachers at any grade level in its elementary, middle, and high schools. As for private schools, it would appear that one minority teacher is employed in a parochial school. At university level, at the time of writing, only five minority people are represented at the local university, of which only two are professors, and it is not certain whether they hold a full professorship, or are assistant professors; none are tenured. Social workers from minority backgrounds are even more scarce. The Department of Children and Youth can boast of having one

African-American social worker in Monroe County at the time of this study—a recent acquisition.

Dr. Lina Giusti took the up question of having service providers who identify with clients who differ from mainstream clientele in her presentation, *Breakpoint and Beyond Youth Violence*, presented at the December, 1994 conference of Walden University doctoral students. She said:

> Considering the principle of diversity, families in need are likely to vary in their characteristics, such as socio-economic status, racial/ethnic group, sexual preference of members, and type of community. Therefore, knowledge of, and sensitivity to cultural diversity issues [are] very important. A requirement for a culturally sensitive service is to conduct an assessment or intervention with the ethnic background of the family members in mind. Diversity among staff members is also significant; both to help other staff members learn different lifestyles and points of view and to provide role models for families in trouble (1994).

This is a very important factor to be considered, particularly as it relates to minority adolescents who are at a stage in their lives when they are very impressionable and need role models to provide examples of what is achievable by members of their own race.

Professional representation in terms of minority members is practically non existent in this area. For example, one African-American psychologist ostensibly services the minority client youth population of the entire Monroe County area. Such a situation bears witness to the necessity for continuing to implement affirmative action legislation and to ensure that it is enforced.

The environment provided by the smaller organizations in rural Pennsylvania for children housed in group homes is little more than that of a holding pen, since group homes function in isolation to the community. The consequence is, that African-American adolescents placed in group homes in non-African-American communities suffer complete social isolation. They have, first of all, been removed from their own community and later find themselves isolated from the community in which the group home is located. This is due to the fact that there are few areas which welcome group homes, regardless of the race of the residents. (See Appendix B.) Additionally, their advisors and counselors are rarely from the same ethnic group. Such conditions portend negative consequences in respect of the adolescents' ability to interact and become part of either their community of origin when released, or the one from which they have been isolated, on reaching legal adulthood. In some instances this has resulted in nervous breakdown.

THE SIGNIFICANCE OF THE STUDY

Each year thousands of minority children are taken into foster care. The outcome of this care, as well as the standard of care, will be unpredictable and poorly documented (Courtney & Collins, 1994, 59). The youths will be removed from families, neighborhoods, friends, schools and communities, under what the researcher has termed "exodus programs." Many adolescents taken into care can expect to spend the remainder of their teenage years away from an environment which is familiar to them. The move to the new environment will be both strange and even more frightening than the inner city (*Neal et al* (*Baby. vs. Robert Casey et al.*, 1992, 55).

Susan Sheehan's biography of Crystal Taylor, *Life for Me Ain't Been No Crystal Stair* (1993), examines this phenomenon, in her description of Crystal's sense of displacement on arriving at the Society for the Prevention of Cruelty to Children in Queensboro, New York:

> Crystal cried on the way there and cried herself to sleep that night. As far as she was concerned, the diagnostic center, situated in a part of the borough of Queens given over to one- and two-family houses with front and back yards, was in the country. 'I wasn't used to dirt ground or little buildings and trees,' she recalls. ' I was used to the city—to Harlem and the South Bronx—and to concrete and projects and high rises and stores within walking distance' (8).

Additionally, the social coping skills which these youths have internalized during their stay in the former environment may prove totally unacceptable to the new (Crittenden & Ainsworth, 1989; Patterson, Capaldi, & Bank, 1991; Patterson & Reid, 1984; Penzerro, 1995). The change for minority adolescents may mean being removed from the African-American community and fostered by middle- or lower-class Euro-American families in a rural environment, or being placed in a group home. In many instances, such families and organizations know little about the culture of the adolescent and deem themselves responsible for the child's welfare only to the extent of meeting minimum needs, preferring to operate foster care as a home business, or as transient shelter.

Magid and McKelvey (1987) discuss the problem of transracial care. Although their focus is on transracial adoption, the same holds true for transracial fostering. They quote one of the directors of the National Association of Homes for Children:

> Transracial adoptions and those which mix ethnic and cultural backgrounds also pose special attachment problems. Said one NAHC director, 'In mixed racial and ethnic minority adoptions, bonding can be a real problem.' He explained that this leads to a failed adoption rate as high as 65%. 'Sometimes neither the agency nor the adoptive family fully understands the genetic, biological and cultural needs of such a child' (152).

The practice of *exodusing* youths is one, which has its origins in the mid-19th century. Charles Loring Brace, founder of the New York Children's Aid Society, developed in 1853 what was then known as the "placing out system." Brace believed the best way to save children was to remove them to rural areas, where farm families could put them to work in an environment deemed morally superior to that of the urban streets (Sheehan, 1993, 20). Hundreds, perhaps thousands, of adolescents removed to these areas run the risk of being psychologically misdiagnosed in terms of their intellectual abilities and mental stability as a consequence of the trauma of abrupt change (Carrier, 1986; Hagan, 1973, Hargreaves, Hester, & Mellor, 1976;

Kaplan & Busner, 1992; Kugelmass, 1987; Mehan, 1983, 1991). They will either find themselves inextricably entrenched in special education classes, or at risk physically in foster or group home environments as a consequence of their participation in programs ostensibly designed by child welfare organizations to protect, or enhance their welfare (Goerge et al. 1994, 537).

According to the American Civil Liberties Union Foundation (1994), approximately 442,000 children in the United States are presently in foster care. Percentages by race and proportion of total child population are given in at Appendix C. Admittedly, while it is preferable to remove an adolescent from an environment where there is the danger of sexual, physical, or psychological abuse, the question remains if whether by reason of overwhelming numbers, the need for expediency, and shortage of staff, adolescents are being thrust into even more dangerous environments (US General Accounting Office, 1993). The average stay of a youth in foster care is 1.4 years. Eleven percent, or 40,600, children are in foster care for 5 years or more; 13% (51,000) for 3-5 years, 16% (59,000) between 2-3 years; and 22% (85,000) between 1-2 years (ACLUF, 1994). The cumulative minimum placement figure for those in care is approximately 6-10 reassignments before the youth leaves the system. If the adolescent is residenced in a group home, s/he may be exposed to other residents who are suffering from a wide spectrum of psychological disorders. These can range in degree of seriousness, from transitory emotional instability, due to the loss of a parent, or post-traumatic distress syndrome as a result of witnessing some form of violence in the home or street; to the more dangerous behaviors of conduct disorder (CD), antisocial personality disorder (APD), or multiple personalities. (MP) (Joint Commission on Mental Health of Children, 1969; Knitzer & Allen, 1978; Knitzer & Yelton, 1990).

There are approximately 28 million adolescents in the United States. Of these, 10% (2,800,000) are categorized as *very high risk* (exhibiting multiple problem behaviors); 15% (4,200,000) are *high risk* (also exhibiting multiple problem behaviors, but to a lesser extent); and 25% (7,000,000) are *moderate risk* (exhibiting one problem behavior). The cumulative figure given for at risk adolescents is 50% (Dryfoos,

1990). According to the Children's Defense Fund's report, *The State of America's Children Yearbook 1997*, of the 4-5 million youths aged 9-17 who have serious emotional problems, fewer than one in four have received treatment recently.

Maughan (1993) and Petrich (1976) report that antisocial personality disorder is heavily represented in the offender population; indications are that rates are as high as 45% of the incarcerated population, as opposed to 7% in the general male population. The peak age for committing crimes is cited by researchers (Wilson and Herrentstein, 1985) as being the early to mid-20s. Conduct disorder, a precondition of APD, is heavily represented in group home residents.

The Fanshel (1990) and Festinger (1983) studies revealed that multiple placements and emancipation from group care, as opposed to leaving family situations, is closely correlated with the incarceration rates of youths. The Stehno study (1987) perceives the foster care system as failing to provide residents with appropriate living skills, thus placing them at further risk for negative outcomes on exiting care.

On February 15, 1995, a local public service television network (WVLT, Pennsylvania) aired a program in which the host spoke with a panel of members from the Department of Children and Youth (C & Y) comprising the Director, David C. Ungerer, Program Specialist, Cheryl Bleiler, and the department's attorney, Patricia Dervish. Director Ungerer began the discussion by stating that in 1995, C & Y in rural Pennsylvania had received $12,000,000 in the form of grants. During the interview it was revealed that 24,000 youths have been referred to Pennsylvania. Of these, 6,755 have been referred to C & Y in the immediate rural area (Allentown, Bethlehem, Easton, and the environs of Monroe County). For the above number of children, C & Y provided only 35 foster homes, of these only 7 were African-American, of which only three were in place, and the balance pending acceptance at the time of this study. The paucity of foster parents in the area confirms the ACLUF finding that the percentage of qualified foster parents has decreased in the United States by 25% since 1984. The 1984 figure of 134,000 has declined to 100,000. Despite the decrease in the number of families available to adopt or foster children of color, the proportion of African-American families who have considered adoption remains high. However, there is a flaw in the system which prevents African-American families from gaining access to these children. According to Mason and Williams (1985) Many African-American families which would consider adoption have been screened out of the process. A study conducted by the National Urban League (Hill, 1993), which followed the progress of 800 African-American families who applied to adopt, revealed that only two were approved for adoption. It is obvious from the foregoing that there is some impropriety in the selection process. Another obstacle, according to the North American Council on Adoptable Children (1991), is that of agency fees and lack of flexibility in terms of criteria used to judge the suitability of African-American families to adopt. As well, the report cites institutional in combination with racist attitudes and lack of minority staff, as other factors impacting the number of eligible African-American adoptive parents. (Rodriguez and Meyer (1990))

The shortage of adoptive/foster parents of African-American descent presents a serious problem, which is exacerbated in the rural areas of Pennsylvania. One consequence is that a major portion of funds designated for child care to C & Y, is used to contract smaller non-profit organizations to assist in providing foster care. These smaller agencies acquire additional funding from organizations like the United Way, from their employees, through voluntary payroll deductions, through rent charged to the families of the residents, and from proposals submitted to state governments, requesting funding.

According to Whittaker and Pfeiffer's (1994) paper, *Research Priorities for Residential and Group Care,* full- and part-time group care programs which were once popular, are being employed less frequently as a result of the withdrawal of approbation by mental health and social service professionals. The result is that there has been a loss of innovation in the existing programs and prediction of failure as to their effectiveness in fulfilling tasks related to appropriate client care. This has resulted in a winding down of this type of service (58). Additionally, cost effectiveness has been a factor contributing to the desire for change. The median cost of congregate child care, per child, per annum is $50,000; per child in foster home care, $17,000; and preventive services per child, $3,000 (ACLUF, 1994).

Over the past decade there has been an increase in the number of children who are now in the care of relatives. More specifically, the majority of these children are in the care of their grandparents. The number of children in kinship care with no parent in the home grew by 75 percent during the first half of the 1990s . The number of children living with no parent present, but in the care of grandparents increased by 66 percent. (CDF, 1997, 55) The question which looms large and threatening, is whether the grandparents will be able to care for these children until they reach the age when they can care for themselves.

III
Literature Review

The review of literature was conducted with a view to tracing the history of African-Americans, to discover how the prevailing conditions came about.

One of the most meaningful words in the English language for the African-American is the word "no," since it is used within the context of both "lack" and "obstruction." Twenty-five years following the abolition of slavery, former slaves were determined to negate some of the "noes" in their lives. In 1890, many attempted to self-repatriate to Africa as passengers on ships headed for Liberia, but were coerced into staying in the United States by Southern agriculturists, who used violence, once they realized the absence of the African-American would result in a severe loss of profits in agriculture.

By the first decade of the 20th century, the war between the farmer and the boll weevil was well underway, and many Caucasian farmers succumbed to the might of the weevil and moved to urban areas, and directly into competition with African-American urban workers (Marks, 1989).

World War I, which formed part of the second decade of the 20th century, halted the flow of immigrants from Europe, thus imperiling the growth of Northern industry. Resolution of the problem was found in the recruitment of African-Americans. They were plentiful, inexpensive, and could not join unions. Therefore, they could not strike for higher wages, or better conditions. In many instances, they were used as strike breakers. Northern migration was both a response and an alternative to the more negative aspects of sharecropping, or poor-paying jobs in southern cities which, combined with social injustice, had been the onus borne by the African-American since arriving in the United States (Marks, 1989).

The living conditions encountered by the southern migrants on their arrival in the North were not those prevalent in large cities today. African-Americans and Caucasians lived side by side until the 1930s. The change was occasioned by two events: the Great Depression and World War II. The first gave impetus to increased African-American Northern migration. The new migrants had borne the onus of financial hardship during the depression and sought relief in the North. Their arrival resulted in a condition of overcrowding and the subdivision of existing accommodation into smaller units (Massey & Denton, 1989).

The second factor contributing to increased segregation and the concentration of African-Americans in inner city areas, was the end of World War II, which brought with it financial prosperity. As a consequence, the US government and industry experienced freedom from the economic constraints which had existed during the depression. Money, which had been used for the war effort, was freed for allocation to building projects. Construction plans which had laid dormant during the depression and the war, and which could not be completed due to lack of manpower and funding, were reactivated. Financial assistance in the form of home loans also became available. Many Caucasians who had been living in restrictive conditions accessed these loans and moved into private housing. The relocation of these individuals left vacant housing in old neighborhoods, which was then made available for African-American expansion. It would be 25-30 years before African-Americans became financially equipped to exodus these areas. This would come as a result of the gains made through the civil rights movement.

The refusal of Rosa Parks on December 1, 1955, to relinquish her seat to a white passenger on a bus in Montgomery, Alabama sparked the commencement of political action which led to a nationwide initiative to extinguish *Jim Crow*. The Rosa Parks incident marked the beginning of a year-long bus strike by African-American passengers in Montgomery, which eventually led to the march on Washington. Such initiatives, in turn, gave rise to the necessity for a recapitulation of earlier legislation and matters concerned with human rights. This, in turn, called for an examination of factors contributing to the birth of a double standard in the United States (Abraham, 1988), in which a condition of dual citizenship existed. The duality perpetuated a situation in which one race lived under separate and unequal conditions, while the other enjoyed the full fruits of freedom (Blauner, 1990).

No longer content to accept second class citizenship as a way of life, the better educated, politically active African-Americans in the North and South began to demand equal rights under the law (Carson, 1987). In the North there was perpetual anger over the fact that once below the Mason/Dixon line, African-American citizens became little more than beings who were at the very best tolerated, and at worse likely to be lynched and raped. Such conditions had prompted the great African-American migration North.

Some 30 years after the march on Selma, Alabama, young people are now beginning to question whether the long-term goals of the civil rights movement will ever be achieved (Bettis, 1994; Sowell, 1984). The disintegration of inner city environments, the covert and often blatant efforts of the Republicans to usurp gains previously made through the civil rights effort, signal a return to an earlier era. The successful attempt by government to nullify affirmative action legislation, and the discontinuance of many community, and building renovation programs initiated prior to the Reagan and Bush eras (Katz, 1989), does not portend well for African-Americans. Additionally, social factors (i.e. the growth of organizations like the skinheads, covert racism experienced by the middle class [Cose, 1993]) have combined to create a sense of hopelessness and discouragement in young men and women living in these areas. The middle class as well has experienced growing pessimism (Urban League, 1994).

For inner city residents without a high school education, prospects look extremely gloomy. In past decades, those who were unable to complete their education were still capable of providing support for their families through participation in blue collar employment, but opportunities for employment in this area have all but disappeared, having been replaced by work in the services industries. The services sector requires that the worker be well educated, thus eliminating many young people from the work force.

This is a particularly debilitating situation, since the median age of the African-American population is approximately 27 years. Therefore, the majority of unemployed African-Americans are in terms of age, at the height of their earning capacity, and also at the stage where they are most likely to need such earnings to support families.

There has been a general outcry against continuing to support welfare recipients, accompanied by allegations of fraud, laziness and the well-known cliché of *welfare mentality,* which assumes that those receiving benefits perceive this way of life as a career. Very little has been mentioned about the working poor, who work at the minimum wage level. Lack of income relegates people in this category to a lifetime of perpetual poverty, and an existence which daily provides the option of choosing between hunger and clothing; and housing and health care. The working poor often make just enough to keep them from becoming eligible for welfare and not enough to cross the poverty line (Ropers, 1991).

The most insidious aspect of poverty for both those on welfare and the working poor is its impact on the health and welfare of minority children. Minority youth are worse off today than they were a generation ago, because they have no sense of community. The success of the civil rights movement led to individuation, a social condition which had not previously existed in the African-American community. Much like the indigenous communities of Africa, earlier African-American communities perceived childcare as a community responsibility. But successful attempts to breach the job market, move to better neighborhoods, and generally gain greater control of life's direction, have resulted in a myopic focus on self (Becnel, 1993).

The loss of the caring community through the exodus of its members to better areas, has resulted in a loss of both community vitality and African-American-owned businesses.

The African-American church, which has traditionally been the foundation of the African-American community, has experienced dwindling congregations—particularly its middle-class parishioners. The loss of the middle class has affected the community in two ways: first, it has resulted in a reduction in community programs; and second, the buffer which existed between poverty and outright destitution has been removed via the exodus of the middle class from these areas (Rubin, 1994).

Recent efforts to change economic conditions in areas like Harlem have resulted in the setting up of street vendors, as a response to the hemorrhaging of capital from this community. This has been received negatively by the police, small business representatives, and city officials, who have desperately tried to extinguish this infant attempt at enterprise (Davidson, 1995). Most amazingly, attempts at street vending, replicate development efforts in Third World countries, where they are hailed as an excellent small scale income-generating initiative. Most Western development organizations encourage this form of self-help in developing countries with funding, advice, education, and even send specialists from the West to assist infant initiatives at this level (Adelman, 1986; Mellor, 1986). However, in economically depressed areas of the United States, the same effort is criticized. Criticism comes in the form of outcries against the potential to use of such business as a cover up for criminal activities, as though this does not occur in the areas where such businesses are being supported by development funds and advice in Third World countries.

The African-American has always believed that education is the key which will open the door to success. During slavery, when it was forbidden to learn to read and write, slaves gathered in the woods to learn how to understand the swirling figures which represented thoughts, at the risk of having their eyes removed or their tongues cut out.

The fruits of the civil rights movement came first to those who, because of their education, were able to take advantage of legislative changes that enabled them to move into positions that were previously closed. In an interview which Nick Chiles (1993) held with Dr. James P. Comer, Professor of Child Psychiatry and Associate Dean at the Yale Medical School, Comer discussed the many saddening statistics regarding the number of minority students suspended annually and the question of increasing educational disillusionment among minority students as they progress from one grade to the next. Rison (1992) agrees with Comer and perceives that under the present conditions, education is little more than an uphill climb in foreign territory for many minority students. Much of what a child achieves in school is dependent on the teacher's perception of his/her ability. In the early stages of education, the child often perceives the teacher as the sole source of wisdom, even to the extent of discrediting parents' views (Payne, 1994).

Winborne and Dardaine-Ragguet's (1993) study of the perceptions of principals in urban schools, as to the needs of urban children in education, revealed that most agreed there was a great need to develop alternatives to traditional curriculum design and instructional approaches. This was necessary because the service provided must accommodate the needs of an ethnically and culturally diverse population.

At present, traditional classroom structures are viewed by these principals as having properties which may negatively affect the maturation of students at risk. In agreement also is Christine Bowditch (1993), who addresses the problem of pushout/dropout. She contends that African-American students experience a significantly higher rate of school suspension than Caucasian students. As well, Bowditch says that many students either drop out or are pushed out of schools because of their incapacity to learn, or what appears to be indifference. (Approximately 1,500 African-American and Hispanic students quit school each day in the United States). Whether a student receives redirection or special attention, very much depends on his/her grades. If s/he is not doing well in class and comes from a family which fits financially into the lower socio-economic bracket, s/he may be either totally ignored, or eventually expelled. Parents of such children have little if any recourse. Because of their economic status they lack the influence or the knowledge necessary to counteract decisions made by the more adept school administration.

Often teachers, together with parents may find it difficult to override the findings of those in administration who hold a more esteemed status, and who, by manipulation of language, can persuade and convince those in decision-making positions to view the student's potential and disabilities from their perspective (Mehan, 1983). This is particularly so in terms of decisions with respect to the school's opinion as to whether a student is in need of special education.

Payne (1994), in her study, *The Relationship Between Teachers' Beliefs and Sense of Efficacy and Their Significance to Urban LSES*

Minority Students, examines the power of the teacher in the classroom to affect student performance. She draws a correlation between teacher attitudes and expectation formation in African-American and Hispanic students.

Kozol (1967, 1991) provides insight into conditions which affect education. His study reveals that education today has become little more than a half promise to those in inner city schools who pursue it. Poorly equipped classrooms, structurally defective buildings, lack of equipment, teachers with poor attitudes, and peer group pressure, all play their roles in pushing the disadvantaged child closer to failure.

For those who have slipped through the cracks and are attempting to recover from an existence of perpetual welfare or crime, the Department of Public Welfare provides training programs. Many of these involve participants who are earnestly seeking a change and others who see minimal attendance as a means of ensuring continued benefits. Such programs do little to shape either the attitudes or social skills of participants. Some vocational programs, such as typing, which endeavor to teach participants to reach a speed of 35 words per minute within six months, lack the requisite (grammar, grooming, presentation, and communication), necessary to ensure that students receive a total founding in the skills necessary to succeed. Many of the participants fail to attend classes, become bored with what is being taught, or being well aware of their other shortcomings, realize their prospects and simply drop out, returning to a life of crime (Auletta, 1983). Their return to previous lifestyles portend negative outcomes for their families and in particular their children. In this instance, the particular focus is on child health.

According to Kirk Johnson (1993), there has been deterioration in health services and health conditions among the minority population which is reaching crisis proportions. A significant number of minority children never live to reach their 18th birthday. African-American babies are dying at twice the rate of Caucasian babies during the first year of life, and the infant mortality rate for African-American babies is higher than that in many developing countries. Nearly one in seven African-American babies is born at a low birth weight and is 40 times more likely to die than a normal weight baby. Accidents in the home are another leading cause of death, and these are 15 times more likely to occur in an African-American home than a Caucasian. Additionally, because many African-American children are on Medicaid (1.5 million are completely uninsured) they are less likely to be immunized.

There remains among the young people who are resident in inner city areas, a pervading sense of futility. Despite the obvious successful efforts of many young African-American children in achieving high academic standards and becoming hardworking individuals, they are perpetually bombarded with negative images of their people in the mass media. Often they as individuals are judged en mass in terms of failure, and as an exception in terms of success, if acknowledged. Judgments of this type have led to stressors in lifestyle, and as a consequence the African-American suffers from high blood pressure and other stress related diseases. While it is true that in some instances the cause can be traced to diet, the stress of racism, poverty and poor living conditions, inadequate education, and a sense of futility, are much more likely to be major factors contributing to poor health (Henderson, 1994). Much of the blame lies in the lap of ambitious politicians and the media, which sensationalize issues surrounding events occurring in African-American communities. It is felt in the African-American community that such sensationalization is effected with a view to increasing readership and audience (Beckett, 1994).

Doris Robinson's (1994) interview with Hazel O'Leary, Secretary of the US Department of Energy (DOE), on January 22, 1993, takes up the question of medical experimentation on African-Americans. Robinson discusses the syphilis experiment which took place in Tuskegee, Alabama, in which African-American veterans were given no treatment for the disease during a longitudinal study to determine the full affect of the disease on human beings. O'Leary also discussed the issue of intentional radiation releases into the atmosphere as experimental practice, which may well have affected over 800 people.

Harriet A. Washington (1994) conducted an investigation which uncovered numerous medical experiments carried out on African-Americans. These ranged from burning them on the arms (Medical College of Virginia) and injecting them with live cancer cells (Sloan-Kettering Institute), to extracting blood from 7,000 boys (National Institute of Health), 95% from underprivileged African-American families. The experiment, which was ostensibly a test for anemia, was actually a blood screening experiment to screen boys with extra "Y" chromosome, which the Institute felt would make them "XYY," and thus more likely to develop criminal attributes than boys having "XY chromosomes. Washington says that the most vulnerable group for experimentation are children, soldiers, and the mentally disabled.

From a psychological perspective, the African-American minority has experienced a further depletion of self-esteem due to the publishing of Charles Murray's (1995) book, *The Bell Curve,* which describes the intelligence of the "average" African-American as being 15% below that of the Euro-American. The heavy emphasis on this aspect of the book's findings which is noted with much alacrity, is not paralleled in Murray's other finding, which reveals the superiority of Asian intelligence over that of the Euro-American. Such biased perspectives arc rarely counterbalanced, or explicated with a view to obtaining a rounded focus on the findings.

Anthony Appiah (1995), a Harvard University professor who is an indigene of Ghana and who took top honors in medical sciences and philosophy at Cambridge University, England, discusses the findings and the inconsistencies in Murray's book and points out that such findings are not new. He states that the study failed to take into consideration many significant variables which might have influenced present findings.

The attempt to negate the intelligence of the African-American and impose a sense of inferiority has been examined by Joseph White (1984). White provides several models of abuse and argues that the attempt to employ Eurocentric methods for gauging intelligence, or in psychological assessment, cannot be successful when working with ethnically different clients. In doing so, he offers a new approach to psychology, from an African-American perspective. Until recently psychotherapeutic treatment was administered to patients of diverse cultural backgrounds without any thought being given to such diversity and its impact on the perceptions of the individual in relation to the world around him (Boyd-Franklin, 1989). A sensitivity to the difference plays a significant role in the psychiatric outcome and the relationship between the clinician and patient. This is particularly so, as it relates to children of color, who by virtue of what has been cited above, perceive the world in much different terms than those who belong to the majority group. Majority group children are less susceptible to many of the health, social, and economic stressors of living in the United States today (Gibbs et al., 1989; Ridley, 1994; Thompson & Jenal, 1994; Trescott, 1995).

One of the first initiatives which must be taken by clinicians, is to try to understand the impact of behaviors and conditions which place adolescents at risk for adverse outcomes. In order to do this, the clinician must be aware of the conditions both social and economic which form part of the environment in which the child lives (Kazdin, 1993; White, 1984).

Within the field of development psychopathology, adolescents have received much less attention than have children. Approximately 17-22% of youth under the age of 18, suffer developmental, emotional, or behavioral problems, which means that 11-14 million of the 63 million suffer significant impairment. Of the approximate 28 million adolescents within the range of 12-17, about 5 million have, or have experienced significant impairment due to an emotional or behavioral problem (Kazdin, 1993).

Cose (1993) reviews the question of the psychological impact of removing adolescents from slum areas. He agrees, that, while placing them in a more wholesome environment could go a long way toward reducing crime, by introducing them to more productive goals, little would be achieved in the area of reducing alienation. In this regard he refers to the plight of the middle-class African-Americans who, in moving away from the ghetto, have not escaped the demon of racist America and consequently remain estranged in a state of emotional turmoil.

William Glasser (1963) contends that youths who suffer from a sense of alienation and consequently carry the heavy onus of guilt, disaffection, and crime, should undergo reality therapy which looks at the treatment of young offenders from the perspective of forgetting about past problems and beginning with a clean slate. It is a sort of "Today, is the first day of the rest of your life" approach. Under the treatment, the offender is told that s/he can no longer blame others for irresponsible acts and that s/he is responsible for his/her own life.

The researcher felt that this would not be an effective way to deal with children who are as seriously affected as those found in foster care. First, because in many instances their present psychological state is the consequence of matters poorly handled by others, and which are significant to their welfare. Therefore, they are virtually not responsible for many facets of their behavior, or their psychological state. Second, psychologically many are not capable of understanding the consequence of specific behaviors, particularly since they have had so few good role models. The reasoning which lies behind the use of this therapy is one that requires higher cognitive and problem-solving skills, which are normally lacking in conduct-disordered adolescents.

Carl Rogers' (1959) theory of personality is premised on an individual's response to his/her environment. He contends that behavior depends on the subjective reality of the respondent and not external reality. The conscious and unconscious are symbolizations of the individual's experiences. Experience may not be correctly symbolized and thus the individual will behave inappropriately. This may take the form of providing responses the subject will require to alienate the recipient.

Sroufe and Waters' (1977) studies of unattached adolescents indicate that they are more likely to misread environmental and interpersonal cues, and become bullies or exhibit behavior which is hostile. Rogers argues that it is important that the subject learn how to read cues correctly.

According to Proctor and Davis (1994), inner city minority groups require psychological intervention which relates to the cultural difference between patients in this category and others. To ignore the difference is to ignore part of the patient's personality. If the clinician is able to relate to his/her patient on these terms, it is more likely that there will be a successful outcome in terms of treatment. It will certainly provide a good deal of insight into their perspective of reality.

Many of the mannerisms observed by clinicians when treating African-American patients are misinterpreted. For example, silence could be misdiagnosed as truculence, when actually, it may be fear or mistrust. Magid and McKelvey (1989) say that mistrust may have its foundation in early unattachment, due to long periods of absence by parents from the child, and the child's inability to form an attachment. The child may also be at risk of maladaptive behavior, such as joining gangs, as a means of belonging; participating in drug-taking activities, as a means of escape; and lastly, criminal activity, as a means of pacifying a sense of rage. Factors of this type have a direct bearing on the contextual reality of the patient and his/her perspective of the world. In turn, it may well be that certain physiological changes occur in the brain to accommodate these factors.

Jane M. Healy's *Endangered Minds* (1990) provides some very convincing evidence which would counter that of Glasser. Her study reveals a correlation between behavior, environment, and the affect of both on the structural capacity and growth patterns of the brain. Such structural abnormalities are occasioned by the failure of specific areas of the brain to develop, due to lack of stimulus. This condition is present in conduct-disordered youths who suffer unattachment.

One of the most dangerous conditions existing in areas where there is a high crime rate, drug use, and overworked single parent and a dysfunctional family, is that of unattachment. Unattachment is a condition in which the child grows up in an atmosphere where there is little closeness between parent and child. This can be as a consequence of the parents having to work for long periods of time, or as a result of institutionalization. Institutionalization at birth, or in the first two years of life can lead to a condition of unattachment. For example, the infant who is institutionalized may, due to lack of adequate staff, spend hours alone in a crib with no one to hold or show it affection. Such children grow up without a sense of belonging and experience no affection (Barth, 1993; Dodge, 1985; Doren, 1987; Henggeler, 1989; Hester & Nygen, 1981; Kagan, 1991; Kazdin, 1987; Magid & McKelvey, 1989; Maughan, 1993; Penzerro & Lein, 1995). Alienation is often further exacerbated by the placement of the minority child in a non-minority home. This is often necessary due to the paucity of minority foster homes available to agencies.

Over the past decade there has been tremendous debate over the question of whether cross-cultural social work and cross-cultural adoption can be successful. The National Association of African-American Social Workers flatly says "No." Less adamant researchers feel that it is possible to develop an understanding and useful relationships at a cross cultural level (Proctor & Davis, 1994; Solomon, 1976). But what about fostering which is not on a one-to-a family basis, but a group home environment?

The real problem begins to surface when minority children are taken out of their community and placed into care. Whittaker and Pfeiffer (1994) focus on the question of group home care, which they perceive as inadequate to the psychosocial needs of adolescents. They argue that such environments fail to provide the skills and interpersonal relationships which will be required when the adolescent reaches adulthood.

According to the *Children's Rights Project: Case Summaries, December 1994*, published by the New York American Civil Liberties Union Foundation, a suit is being conducted against the state of Pennsylvania on behalf of approximately 6,000 children in Philadelphia's foster care system. The plaintiffs contend that the defendants are violating plaintiff's federal constitutional, and federal and state statutory rights, by failing to provide the plaintiff children with legally mandated services. The plaintiffs' contention supports the researcher's view that the present system may be more deleterious to child welfare than helpful.

Courtney and Collins (1994) perceive the problem as lying in poorly monitored data, which prevents agencies from being fully apprised of many significant factors affecting the clients in their care. Some controversy has also been generated in area of foster care. Courtney and Collins question the capacity of group homes to provide youths with skills and adequate nurturing which will be beneficial to them in developing the necessary attitudes to produce individuals who are capable of contributing to their communities and society in general.

Mech (1994) states in, *Foster Youths in Transition: Research Perspectives on Preparation for Independent Living*, that the transition period from late adolescence to early adulthood, is critical to the course of human development. This period is categorized as covering the years from age 17-22. Mech further finds, based on his study, that a successful outcome of this transition cannot occur in a social vacuum and requires a balanced input of social competence, self-direction, adequate self-esteem, living skills, and the ability to interact competently with others, as well as having sufficient exposure to community organizations and religious institutions.

Agreeing with Mech, Stehno's (1987) study, *Kaleidoscope's Youth Development Program: A Last Chance for Youth "Aging Out of Foster*

Care, perceives the services provided for youth in group homes as being unable to provide residents with adequate living skills which they will require for independent living. In this regard, Stehno describes the adolescent population in this category as 60% male and having experienced as many as 1-29 foster placements, the median being 11. Adolescents are also cited as suffering from low esteem, having behavioral problems and a large proportion, as illiterate.

The need for affective fostering is also a significant factor in achieving a positive outcome for adolescents who leave public care. Solid relationships which provide youths with a sense of being a part of the family by which they are fostered is crucial to positive welfare outcomes.

Barth's (1993) *On Their Own: The Experiences of Youth After Foster Care,* examines the need for affective fostering. His study reveals that nearly 90% of the adolescents who leave foster care for independent living continue to maintain contact with their former foster parents, or group homes after they leave, at a rate of approximately five times a year. The youths studied also stated that they intend to continue contact. The study brings into question the appropriateness of existing social work and educational practices which encourage caregiver/client or teacher/student distancing. This practice has been cited as harmful by adolescent specialists, in the fields of education and psychology (Comer, 1988; Haynes, 1993; Kozol, 1967; Magid & McKelvey, 1987; McWhirter, 1993; Penzerro & Lein, 1995; Rutter, 1993).

Contradicting the perspective of the above theorists are Elliot and Ageton (1980), and Elliot, Ageton, Huizinga, Knowles, & Carter (1983), have written two papers on the results of the National Youth Study which was conducted on delinquent youths. The study consisted of a list of behavioral items which were designed to discover the philosophies, opinions, and directions of these adolescents. Elliot and his colleagues conducted a later study in 1989, and found that while the latest findings revealed significant results in respect of measures of moral beliefs about breaking the law and peer association, it revealed nothing that would indicate a variability in behavior as a reflection of attachment, goal commitment, and involvement in conventional activities. The findings, however may be contestable on the grounds of "subject expectation formation," in other words, the provision by the subject of a reaction which s/he believes the interviewer anticipates receiving.

Additionally, it could be that the subjects participated in these activities for too brief a period to be influenced. If, however, the Elliot findings are replicated, then it may mean that the present psychological condition of many adolescents is one which is intractable. Certainly, it would appear that further research into this matter is required.

To summarize, the literature review begins with historical and political events which led to the problems which are now prevalent in the inner city. Cited in this section of the literature review were Abraham (1988); Blauner (1990); Bettis (1994); Carson, Garrow, Haring & Hine (1987); Massey & Denton (1989); Redkey (1969); and Sowell (1984), who cover the history of the African-American from 1890, 27 years after the abolition of slavery to the present, by discussing the different methods employed by former slaves to free themselves of laws such as the *Black Codes*, which restricted their mobility and kept them in a state little better than that of slavery. Abraham (1988) and Carson et al. (1987) provide a sequential review of the civil rights movement to abolish *Jim Crow* and establish more equitable conditions for African-American citizens. Abraham's study takes an inside look at the legislation used to support the civil rights initiative and the redrafting of legislation to change prohibitive regulations.

Katz (1989) conducts a follow up which scrutinizes post civil-rights programming and the disintegration of state and government programs designed to assist the inner city poor. It begins with the war on poverty and concludes with the war on welfare. He describes the initiatives taken before and after the Reagan and Bush eras, citing two factors—(a) disruption of state and federal community programs, and (b) loss of employment in the unskilled sector—as having played a significant role in the creation of growing pessimism among African-Americans. As a consequence, Sowell (1984) contends that many former supporters of civil rights and activists themselves have been led to question the successful outcome of civil rights initiatives. Many see the civil rights movement as one which benefited only the middle class, while others feel that even these benefits are being slowly eroded through legislation covertly enacted to nullify, or at the very least weaken, the strengths of former gains.

In Ellis Cose's (1993) *Rage of a Privileged Class*, the reader is given an inside look at the covert discrimination which middle class African-Americans suffer in silence as they struggle to hold on to their newly acquired status in positions which are ostensibly at decision-making levels in corporate structures. Some of the frustrations associated with "getting a piece of the pie" include not being able to join "the club," not being consulted about decisions which affect their departments, gender bias and lastly, "the glass ceiling."

Feagin and Imani's paper (1994), *Racial Barriers to African-American Entrepreneurship: An Explanatory Study*, focuses on the question of glass ceiling and the many obstacles that African-Americans have to face when going into business. The matter of economics and the impact of out-migration of the middle class from the inner cities were also examined as additional factors contributing to the increased negative environment. This portion of the literature review examined the unfolding of political and social activities, which led to the decline of the inner cities and provides some observations as to why unemployment is so much higher in these areas than in other parts of the United States.

As a follow up to the above topics, the review focused on the question of inner city poverty, its causes, and its impact on residents. Resources for this section were taken from works by Richard H. Ropers (1991), whose book, *Persistent Poverty: The American Dream Turned Nightmare*, and Schwarz and Volgy's (1992) offering, *The forgotten American*, examine the plight of the working poor. Both authors employ the statistics of economics to reveal a close resemblance in the economic condition in America and many third world countries. Ropers states that during the period 1978-1987, the bottom one fifth of the population's share of income declined by 8%, while the income of the top one-fifth increased by 13%. Ropers also investigates the question of welfare fraud and concludes from his findings that there is greater evidence to support the claim that most of the abuse occurs at the administrative level.

Barbara Becnel's (1993) article, *Poverty as Policy* looks at poverty's impact on children in terms of health, education and future prospects. Her view is that African-Americans, and particularly women, suffer because they are hampered in freedom of movement and expression by their overwhelming dependence on the whims of government. Poverty further impacts children socially as a group. She says that in this context, African-American children are worse off than they were a generation ago because they have no sense of community. Today, the African-American community is not a socially cohesive entity. In the past, people tended to be dependent on one another. However, they do not feel as responsible for one another today, and in this regard she places the blame on the civil rights movement, which through its success, has made people feel less threatened by the racial situation and hence less obligated to uplift one another. In consequence, they tend to act, work, and achieve independently. Prior to civil rights, African-Americans were forced to depend on one another and therefore took responsibility for the welfare of one another's children. She goes on to say that the heavy reliance on government programs—which were initially brought into existence through the civil rights movement—has allowed for the acceptance of programs which have structurally related stipulations that are restrictive and too inflexible to meet the changing needs of society.

Massey & Denton 's (1993) *American Apartheid* and O'Hare's (1991) *African-Americans in the 1990s* perceive a number of factors as having combined to exacerbate the existing poverty in inner cities. First, there is the loss of blue-collar employment, which has led to a condition where male heads of household are unable to support their families. This situation has been further aggravated in the past by public welfare programs such as Aid to Families with Dependent Children, which prohibit dependent mothers from cohabiting with the fathers. The penalty for doing so may still mean taking a chance on being dropped from the public support program. The change in the nature of employment from blue collar to a growth in positions in the services industries was followed by the exodus of the middle class to the suburbs as a consequence of the middle class obtaining better paying jobs through affirmative action. To obtain these jobs, the middle class also moved to the sunbelt areas like Silicon Valley, where higher paying employment was available to qualified African-Americans.

Rubin (1994), in his paper *The Role of the African-American Church in Working with Adolescents,* agrees with Massey et al. (1993) and O'Hare (1991), adding that the consequence of the exodus, was a loss of community support for programs which historically had been provided through the African-American church. Rubin provides tables derived from his studies which reveal a direct correlation between the size of the middle class congregation and the number and type of youth programs available.

Additionally, Davidson (1995) contends that inner cities have always been victim to a siphoning off of community wealth by traders and merchants who do not identify culturally or demographically with the residents. The outflow of these funds has been responsible for a good deal of the existing poverty, since the funds go to communities outside the areas from which they have been obtained and thus are not reinvested into the community. The section on health focused on some of the consequences of poverty in the inner city and its impact on the lives and health of children and others who are disadvantaged or powerless to defend themselves, such as the mentally ill. Johnson (1993) states that health programs are poorly designed in terms of providing service, continuity and homogeneity in inner city areas. Such a situation has led to a decline in the general health of minority children, who suffer mouthfuls of rotten teeth, are poorly immunized, and who would be totally uninsured were it not for Medicaid.

Robinson (1994) and Washington (1994) contend that experiments like the syphilis experiment conducted on African-American males, have led to the belief by many African-Americans, and particularly males, that they are being systematically exterminated. This in turn, has manifested in African-Americans, a reluctance to participate in any medical programs (immunization included). Those groups most vulnerable to experimentation are children, veterans, and the mentally disabled. According to Washington's study, large numbers of African-American prisoners have also been used to conduct various types of medical experiments.

The review also covered the question of African-American psychology, both as an intervention method and as a discussion of the African-American psyche. The psychological impact of nature and nurture on minority group members was the concern of the writers cited in this section. The contributing writers have discussed techniques from many different aspects. Technical strategies covered approaches which ranged from the "Today is the first day of the rest of your life," the need for culturally relevant counselors, to structural changes in the brain as a factor impacting the capacity to learn and adhere to appropriate behavior.

Lastly, the literature review took up the question of out-of-home care and its impact on inner-city youths who have been removed from their homes, communities and families. According to Whittaker and Pfeiffer (1995), group home care and institutionalization are not the most effective means of caring for young people who require the services of public welfare. In many instances, poorly planned care can be more harmful than helpful. Present-day services need to be revised to look at the question of providing guidance which will assist the child to become a fully functioning individual upon reaching legal adulthood.

While foster parenting is viewed by many social workers as far more beneficial in terms of providing a homelike environment, numerous placings can prove to be just as deleterious as group home or institutional living for the youth. The multiple placements also known as *streeting* can range between 11-29, before the youth leaves foster care.

The literature review sought to provide the reader with a comprehensive study of the background, social life, living conditions, health, and psychological profile of inner-city youths. This was done with a view to assisting the reader to better understand the impact of sudden change in environment on youths and to provide some insight into why the behaviors, attitudes and perceptions of inner-city youths are different from those of young people from other sectors of society.

IV
Presentation and Analysis of the Data

FOSTER CARE

The study was undertaken with a view to discovering whether mismanagement in the Department of Human Services in Pennsylvania and the child protection services existed, and if so, what affect it had on the provision of service to youths, foster parents, and educational environments. Information was derived from secondary sources, interviews, questionnaires, the researcher's observations while working in two group homes and special education classrooms, as well as discussions with co-counselors and others in the human services area.

The researcher opens this chapter of the study with a description of the experiences of foster youths in group home care, foster care, and classroom environments. The case studies the researcher is about to provide focus on the experiences of two African-American adolescents from inner city areas who were placed in care in rural Pennsylvania. Although the four major case studies are monofocal from the perspective of the race of the residents, the researcher feels that it is necessary to add that in addition to these cases, which describe the abuse of four African-American youths in care, two other residents in care at the group home of the subjects were also removed from the group home for psychiatric assessment, after exhibiting behavior which was inappropriate.

The first was a White female adolescent, approximately 15 years old, whose name the researcher gives as Shelley. Shelley was taken into police custody when she lost her temper and put her fist through the wall during an argument, which took place on a Friday evening, after a week of relentless pressure from a male counselor. The counselor, a retired New York policeman, was accustomed to dealing with hardened criminals. Shelley was taken for psychological assessment, but it was later decided to place her in an adult correctional facility over the weekend. (This was done; it was said, "to teach her a lesson.") Her case was heard the following Monday, at which time she appeared in court chained hand and foot.

The second case was that of a young Hispanic male who also was removed from the residence for doing exactly the same thing. He was kept in the hospital for psychiatric assessment, as opposed to being incarcerated. The action taken by the counselors which led to both acts of frustration was that of refusing to allow both residents the right to listen to their radios, as punishment for a minor infringement. In both instances the counselors refused to disclose to the residents the period for which the punishment would be in effect. Their radios were simply taken away. In both cases the residents had received traumatic news prior to having their property removed. The boy's mother had just told the him, that she no longer wanted him, preferring to continue her homosexual relationship with her friend. The girl had been told that she might not be able to continue to visit her father. Punishment of indeterminate length is tantamount to mental cruelty, as even in prison, prisoners are advised of the period during which they will be under punishment for specific infringements.

Within a period of seven months, three residents had to be taken for psychological assessment. During this period the researcher both observed and was advised of the mental deterioration of the four residents, and noted the diminished capacity of the two youths mentioned above, to interact with the staff prior to the above described incidents. The 24-year-old director of the group homes, who had no children and had never been married, attributed the psychological deterioration of the four residents to "institutionalization." Responsibility had been given to her for the care and assessment of children suffering from various degrees of mental illness, emotional and behavioral problems. At the time these observations were made, the residents were less than 7-9 years younger than the group home director

At group home I, with the exception of a few counselors, there was very little conversation between residents and staff, of a personal nature. Conversation basically took the form of questions which focused on specific instructions. For example the counselor would ask, "Have you made your bed?" "Is this the day you see the psyche?" Did you get a new prescription?" Oral contact of this nature is strictly work-related. As a consequence, counselors were orally abused by residents, who emphatically exclaimed, it was "none of their business." Conversely, those counselors who took the time to ask the residents about their school day, friends, and experiences at school or work, were rarely ostracized.

The following are case studies of two residents who were in care during the period that the researcher worked in the two group homes. The names of the two adolescents and identifiable features have been changed to protect their privacy. Thus, race and age and sex are the sole descriptions provided.

MARLENE

September 10, 1994

The researcher met Marlene for the first time today. She is an African-American girl of approximately 13 years of age. This is her second stay. She was referred to this organization by the Department of C & Y and was initially placed in group home I for girls, which accommodates up to four residents. She is now in group home II. There were three other girls living in the home, one of whom left Wednesday, having attained the age of 18. The other, Shelley, is 15 and like Marlene, is to be accommodated on a long-term basis. Marlene is cheerful, friendly, and open, despite her very painful past. She is the youngest of three children and the only girl. She has two older brothers, ages 18 and 17.

She came to us initially, as a referral from another agency in July, on the death of her mother. At that time, she was accommodated in the sister group home I. Approximately two weeks after the commencement of her residency, she and her two brothers were released into the custody of her late mother's friend, in compliance with the stipulations of her mother's will. This arrangement lasted a little less than one month. The guardian, whom Marlene calls "Auntie," took the three children to an inner city area, where she lived with them in apartment. At the expiration of the aforementioned period, the guardian announced that she simply no longer wanted to care for them, and put them all into the street in the middle of the night in a rather questionable area. The three adolescents somehow managed to return to the home in the Pennsylvania, which their mother had been in the process of buying before she died of a heart attack in July.

Drawing on the rather inconsistent report of Marlene, it appears that the mother, who at the time of her death was 53, had for more than a year endeavored single-handedly to provide for the children and pay the mortgage on her home. Marlene said that her mother's purpose in taking on this heavy financial obligation was to remove her children from the threatening environment of the inner city. However, Marlene and her brothers were not too pleased with the prospect of moving to the sleepy environs of rural Pennsylvania and felt that it was unfair they had not been allowed to participate in the decision-making process. However, upon their return to their Brooklyn, after death of their mother, they did not see the urban environment in the same light.

It was to the home in rural Pennsylvania, that they returned on being pushed into the street. After a few days residency in the family home, Marlene and her 17-year-old. sibling were returned to the custody of C & Y, which had been advised that they were no longer at "Auntie's" house, and abandoned and unsupervised, had returned to the home owned by their mother.

On September 9th, both Marlene and her 17-year-old. brother were withdrawn from their classrooms and advised that someone had come to collect them. Neither knew who it could be. Marlene was assigned to a group home II, under the care of this organization. Her 17-year-old brother was accommodated a great distance away. The eldest, being 18 years old, was given no special assistance and left to his own devices. He is in a particularly vulnerable situation since he cannot live in the family home once the annual taxes become due on the house. The Department of C & Y has taken no responsibility for his welfare, since

18 is the cut off age for children coming under the care and protection of the child protection services.

On the researcher's initial meeting with Marlene, she was somewhat apprehensive and opened a little after observing the rapport the researcher has with the other residents. Marlene appears much older than her 13 years. As a first step in settling her into the home, her clothes were inventoried, washed, and put away. The researcher observed from her clothing, that she has spent a great deal of her life away from the guidance of her mother. She also exhibits poor living skills. At 13, she still sucks her thumb, sleeps in her clothing, and exhibits poor eating and nutritional habits. Her eating skills require a good deal of correction; she slurps her soup and eats solid foods with a spoon, which she also uses to cut her steak.

Her hair and skin are in need of a good deal more care. Her clothing reflects the absence of adult direction and appears to have been selected on the basis of style, without consideration given to appropriateness. As a consequence the majority of her clothing upon arrival consists of shorts—a choice of apparel totally inappropriate for her. Her undergarments are also inappropriate, and it is apparent that no guidance has been given in this respect as concerns the necessity of wearing stockings and undergarments specifically designated for use by females during special times of the month.

Marlene does not wear shoes, but restricts her footwear to sneakers, which do not provide adequate support for someone of her stature. This, in turn, affects her carriage and she appears to be rolling along. Despite the uncleanness of her outer and underwear, Marlene bathes regularly and uses deodorant.

She gets along well with the other residents, follows directions and complies with all the house rules. Her rather tragic past and bleak prospects for the future in respect of her family life with her other siblings has not daunted her optimism, and she exhibits no outward signs of depression. The researcher, however, is concerned because she had not been offered any bereavement counseling which is required in order to assist her in releasing the pent up anger which accompanies the death of a loved one. However, at this time, she is friendly and participates in all group activities, like Ping-Pong, pool, and group walks. I have been unable to get the director to get Marlene some decent clothing.

Marlene is very open in discussing with the researcher the trials in her past and her aspirations for the future. However, the researcher notes that she has a tendency to fantasize about male friends and to match romantic experiences with those of the other two girls. In doing so, Marlene hopes to prove her equality of attractiveness with the other two girls, who are Caucasian. This is not a situation brought about by the racial difference between herself and the other two residents, but merely a "girl" thing, which is done so as not to be seen as being sexually less attractive than the other two. As regards her racial awareness, she is neither overly sensitive about her color, or theirs. She appears to be very comfortable with the researcher, but likes her Caucasian counselors as well, and hugs them when they arrive at the group home, expressing genuine affection.

Her religious training, a very significant factor in African-American cultural identity, appears minimal and her lack of religious training is almost amusing. For example, she thinks that, "Merry Christmas" is actually "Mary Christmas," Mary being Christ's mother. These are the researcher's initial observations on the first day of her stay. The researcher will return tomorrow, and again next week to see whether there have been any changes in her behavior at the close of the first week of her residency.

September 11, 1994

The researcher had an opportunity to spend the day with Marlene . Her behavior remains stable. She continues to be amiable, compliant, and very warm. She is very eager to be accepted. She showed some sadness when talking about her plans for Christmas, stating that she had no place to go. No member of her family wanted to take her over the holidays. This situation was brought to the attention of the program office.

When the researcher directed the conversation to the shopping excursion, which is to take place sometime this coming week, to buy her new clothes, her mood brightened. (No prospect of bereavement counseling for this child is evident).

September 12, 1994

The researcher observed Marlene 's behavior between the hours of 3:00 p.m. and 11:00 p.m. She appears to have settled in and is very much at home. This new-found security has had a profound effect on her behavior. Where she was initially responsive and compliant, she has become belligerent and prone to do what she feels is best, irrespective of instructions from the counselors (Of course this may be a reaction to the loss of her mother.) No one has done anything about bereavement counseling. The change in her behavior within such a short period of time is astounding. In many cases she takes her lead from Shelly, a co-resident, who was placed in the home because she was diagnosed as conduct disordered. Shelly is approximately 2.5 years older than Marlene, and Marlene copies her behavior. Shelley's often-immature behavior has prompted her enrollment in a special education class.

With regard to Marlene, the researcher feels that she may well be of normal intelligence, but this is obscured by regressive behavior, such as thumb-sucking, which the researcher believes is an attempt to return to a more stable period in her life. Her language skills and enunciation, which are a manifestation of her inner city environment, make her appear less intelligent than she is to her counselors. Often they ask me to translate. The researcher found her quite capable of learning and she might have been readily placed in mainstream classes were it not for these liabilities, which reflect badly on her capacities and, in turn, appear to motivate her behavior.

Another manifestation of Marlene 's adapting to her new environment, is that a number of rather offensive habits have begun to emerge, such as talking back, walking around half dressed and, more unnerving, the tendency to belch very loudly. She also speaks at the top of her voice all the time. When asked to lower her voice, she simply responds, "Everyone in my family speaks loud," as if that is justification for this behavior. She has also become very contrary, and exhibits attitudes and responses which are symptomatic of having lived among the lowest classes of society (i.e. a stiff-necked, non-responsive attitude when called; uncooperativeness; and perpetual complaint.) Complaints are made about something as simple as being asked to leave the bathroom after a 15 minute shower, to her obvious lack of appropriate clothing. (In regard to complaining, the researcher is reminded of her own behavior after the death of her mother. The child still has not been provided with bereavement counseling.) The researcher will observe her again in approximately four days, to determine if the rebelliousness is a delayed reaction to her mother's death.

September 23-24, 1994

The researcher saw Marlene on both days and noticed deterioration in her mental stability. Although she continues to be quite amiable, she confessed that she has an obsession with guns. The researcher had a rather long talk with her on the 23rd, during which she spoke to the researcher of having "bad dreams." The one which she remembers most vividly, is one in which her brother is shot with a gun and she is determined to avenge his death.

She also advised the researcher that she has joined two gangs, one group called "the P----" and the other called "B------." She says that she has two forms of initiation, of which one can be chosen. The first is to shoot someone with a gun; the second is to have sex with all of the P--s ten male members. The researcher senses she has joined to fulfill her need to have a family. The period between her mother's death and her arrival here, during which Auntie rejected her, is beginning to unnerve her, and she is exhibiting signs of depression. Outwardly her behavior toward the researcher, is almost normal, but she is preoccupied with guns, of which she speaks almost incessantly, revealing an inner sense of morbidity.

She says that she is a former resident of the ghetto and, being so, it is impossible to change her, remarking that "You can take the child out of the ghetto, but cannot take the ghetto out of the child." The researcher has responded to this on each occasion with a reminder that the researcher, too, was born and grew up in the ghetto. Each time the researcher responds in this manner, Marlene appears somewhat astonished.

On asking her what she wanted to do with her life, she explained to the researcher that she was interested in becoming a teacher, or a lawyer. The researcher asked her if she thought that a teacher or a lawyer could work at their professions having been convicted of shooting someone. This gave her some cause for reflection. She then said that she would like to leave the gang, but was afraid that she would be hurt if she told this to members. The researcher felt that this was just an evasive tactic and that probably the entire story was a figment of her imagination. However, whether true or not, it is not a good indication of her emotional state. The researcher recommended a long period of psychotherapy, but it appears that this organization only supports this type of intervention financially to the order of one-half hour a week of psychoanalysis, carried out by non-African-American psychologists, who have no inner city experience. Of course, even this option may not be available. The researcher feels that this child, who is truly disadvantaged, requires the services of an African-American psychologist who is aware of inner city conditions and the control gangs have over their members.

The researcher's co-worker advised that Marlene received a telephone call yesterday from a relative, before the researcher arrived. During the course of the conversation Marlene became very agitated, stating that she would find the friend of her mother's who put them into the street, get a gun, and shoot her. The co-worker's observation was that as she spoke she paced up and down and exhibited through posturing, a state of high irritability and disquiet

September 25, 1994

By the time the researcher arrived at work today, Marlene appeared perfectly normal and was in the process of carrying out her chores and listening to the radio. All signs of the previous day's irritability and preoccupation with killing were gone.

The researcher would like to do so much for this child, because the researcher understands what she is coming from and how the exodus into a White, middle-class/lower-class society can be threatening. There is nothing here for her relate to. The majority of the residents are White, as are the counselors. Marlene has no foundation upon which she can stand to catch her equilibrium. The researcher has for quite some time, been the only African-American counselor in either of the two houses. The inappropriateness of this situation was not apparent to the director, because until just recently there hadn't been any minority children. The situation has changed, the organization has two, Marlene and one child in the other group home. There is also the possibility that there will be more. These children will have nothing to relate to. (Marlene still has not received any bereavement counseling.)

During the last few days, the researcher spent most of her time at the other house, but was kept apprised of Marlene's behavior, which is said to be deteriorating. She is no longer as open as she had been previously. The researcher has decided to return to group home II, where Marlene is residenced, as soon as feasible, to see what is taking place.

October 6, 1994

Marlene saw the researcher's car pulling into the driveway and began shouting "Here comes my Mom, here comes my Mom." The researcher feels it is a good sign, because the researcher wants to help Marlene to retain her capacity to love. So many children separated from their mothers lose their capacity to love. Between maternal separation and the separation from the community, children live in isolation. Isolation of this type produces an attitude in which young adults learn to care very little for what is happening to them or others, and are capable of committing a crime without the least bit of conscience. The researcher feels that Marlene could be saved if the researcher could only get her to care about every facet of her life.

The researcher noted a change in Marlene. While she was not always co-operative with the other counselors, for the most part the researcher has had little trouble with her. The researcher feels is because traditionally, in African-American culture, mothers and daughters are normally very close, there being in most instances no male head of household. In such situations, mothers and daughters bear the responsibility for the care of other family members. Marlene and the researcher can both relate to this situation. The researcher discussed this aspect of life with Marlene, and how it affected the manner in which life is perceived, as well as the way in which one perceives others.

Marlene was very much upset by the removal of Shelley from the group home. Shelley was an adolescent whose intelligence was considered to be below average. The researcher feels this conclusion might have been reached because her reading and math levels were low. However, the researcher noted that she was capable of learning by heart every single pop song which was played on the radio without ever writing down a word. This leads the researcher question the validity of the findings that her intelligence was low. The researcher would argue that instead, her learning has been "misdirected." In this regard more attention could well have been directed, not to what the she had learned, but how she had learned it. Shelley was interested in "hip hop" songs, so she learned them quickly and correctly. The fact that she was capable of learning them without writing or studying would seem to the researcher, to indicate that she was reasonably intelligent. Additionally, the researcher believes that those assessing her were further biased by her speech impediment.

The researcher did not know how Shelley's absence would affect Marlene. On Shelley's departure, the organization placed two boys in the residence, who were to take the rooms left vacant by Shelley and the other resident who left on her 18th birthday. As the researcher understands it, this is illegal. Group homes are not supposed to house different sexes in a single residence. However, Marlene was unable to return to the group home I residence because the White, female residents refused to sleep in the same room with her. One of the residents in the group home has even posted a White supremacist newspaper on the billboard in her room.

The manner in which Marlene is treated, and the blatant racism with which she was forced to contend, is very difficult for the researcher to understand. The prevailing attitude about Marlene is negative. The researcher's approach to her differs from the way she is treated by the others. The researcher tries to provide her with a strong role model. On the first meeting, the researcher advised Marlene, "When you see me, just consider yourself as being back in your own community—you know what that means." Before the researcher met Marlene the she had been warned by the director that Marlene was very difficult. The researcher responded to this by saying, "No, she isn't either, because I won't put up with that. She knows her culture." The researcher never had any trouble with Marlene.

Earlier today, the researcher had a talk with the co-counselor who advised that Marlene had been making a lot of sexual gestures and connotations in front of the two boys. The researcher said she would talk to Marlene about it, since it appeared that the White counselor was afraid of her. The researcher had a long discussion about what was appropriate and inappropriate behavior for a young lady. Marlene wants to be a "lady," but the environment from she has come, doesn't hold such behavior in very high esteem. It is more appropriate to "act out," to fail, to be sexually promiscuous, or thrill seeking in her former environment. Her sense of isolation and her attempt to get attention have exacerbated the behaviors. There is no African-American community nearby. (No bereavement counseling has yet been given to her, despite the fact that the researcher has written in the log that the child is thinking about joining a gang, having group sex, etc. Instead, the director called the school to find out whether such a gang existed. What did she think the response was going to be from the school, particularly in light of the fact that state funding for the school is at least partially premised on how safe the school environment is for its pupils?)

October 7, 1994

This was a pretty uneventful day. The co-counselor advised the researcher that Marlene has stopped discussing guns and gangs, but has continued to make sexually explicit comments to the two boys living with her in the group home. One of the boys, is a very attractive Latino of about 13, who no doubt will be very handsome when he is grown.

Marlene was rather subdued today. She is supposed to visit her mother's grave tomorrow. (Still no bereavement counseling.) The researcher told her that she would be working on Christmas, so even if Marlene didn't have anywhere to go over the holidays, she would have a friend with her. The researcher told Marlene that they would be going shopping for Christmas presents for the other employees and residents in group home I.

October 9, 1994

The co-counselor warned the researcher that Marlene was not in a very good mood. Yesterday turned out to be an emotional disaster Marlene was driven to New Jersey where her mother's grave is. On the way she bought a lovely bunch of daisies. The counselor got lost, and spent most of the day trying to find the cemetery. When she and Marlene arrived, it was late afternoon and threatening to get dark. To make matters worse, they could not find the grave site because there was no headstone. They searched but could not find it before it got dark. So, they drove all the way back to Pennsylvania, Marlene still holding the flowers. The researcher wondered as she listened, "How much more can this child stand before she has a nervous breakdown?" (Still no bereavement counseling.)

The researcher went down to Marlene's room. From a distance the researcher could see through the open door a large bunch of daisies sitting in a tin can on her dresser. The researcher decided as she walked to Marlene's room that she would not mention the trip, but simply state how beautiful the flowers were, in the event that Marlene wanted to say something about how she felt about the failed trip.

Later that afternoon Marlene began making sexual gestures to the boys and on several occasions the researcher had to tell her to stop. The co-counselor was afraid to tell her anything because she was belligerent. The researcher had brought a copy of the video *Ladyhawk* which Marlene appeared to enjoy. She and the two boys decided to shoot pool in the recreation room. The researcher did not bother to follow them into the room as she could hear them quite well. After a few minutes, the co-counselor went and found Marlene kissing one of the boys. The two, having been caught in the act, immediately blamed one another. The other boy slipped out of the room before the trouble began and remained a safe distance away.

On being accused by the co-counselor, Marlene went into a tantrum, which scared the co-counselor, and the researcher was left with trying to calm her down. During the eruption Marlene threatened to shoot the other resident, who, because of his mental state, threatened back. The researcher took Marlene out of the house in an effort to calm her down, and after some time this was accomplished.

Over the remainder of the period that the researcher worked with the organization she kept in contact with Marlene, despite the fact that she was not always assigned to group home II. When she decided to leave, she asked for permission to visit and work with Marlene on a voluntary basis. This request was denied. The researcher placed the request in the hands of the Departments of Public Welfare, Health and Human Services, the Human Rights Commission. Nothing ever came of the request. During the interim, Marlene's behavior began to deteriorate, once she found that the researcher would not be allowed to continue working with her. She became abusive, hostile, and extremely uncooperative. She refused to be placed in any of the available foster homes, after an attempt by the organization to reassign her. This was due in part to the fact that the organization wanted to place her in a home where she had previously lived. Her experience there was clouded by an issue of sexual abuse, or sexual contact, which was never clarified. At this juncture she assumed an attitude which would ensure that she would not be accepted in that home. Her behavior continued to deteriorate during her stay at the group home, and she began fighting the counselors and making racial slurs. All of this could have been avoided if the organization had been willing to let the researcher work with her on a "non-pay" basis on alternate weekends.

Marlene was sent to summer camp where she spent part of the summer. Upon her return she was placed in an orphanage, since no one wanted to adopt her. She was a child who could have been salvaged, but because of organizational regulations which prevented client/employee contact after the employee has left the organization, she has now become institutionalized and indifferent. After a year of writing, phoning, petitioning on behalf of this girl, the Human Rights Commission finally contacted the researcher and asked whether the researcher wanted to continue action on this case. The researcher requested that the case be dropped because of the extremely long reaction time to the problem and also because the researcher thought she had discovered, on her own initiative, another way to assist the girl. However, the director of group home I had phoned the orphanage and told officers there not to allow the researcher visitor privileges. The DPW, which was the initial department of contact by the researcher, has never responded as regards the result of its negotiations with the group home on Marlene and the researcher's behalf. The investigator never contacted the researcher again, after his initial meeting with her, three years ago.

ACLUF—Reflective Case Study I

Reflecting the same type of situation is the case of Sherry G., who, unlike Marlene, resides in a large urban area of Pennsylvania. Sherry G. is cited by the ACLUF in its action against the Commonwealth of

Pennsylvania Department of Public Welfare (DPW). Sherry G. is an 11-year- old, who first came to the attention of the Department of Public Welfare in September, 1986. At that time, her mother, Mary, and her boyfriend had been accused of sexually abusing Sherry's younger sister, Memphis, by among other things, placing a belt buckle in her vagina that had to be surgically removed.

Sherry, Memphis, and two younger siblings, Jay Jr. and Vickie, had previously lived with their father, Jay G., but in August, 1986, he committed suicide by shooting himself in the head. The children saw the father's body on the floor in a pool of blood before he was taken away. After the father's death the children were sent to live with their mother and her boyfriend in a shelter. During her stay at the shelter, Memphis was sexually abused by her mother and her boyfriend. Sherry and her two other siblings were physically abused. The two adults were subsequently convicted of child abuse and incarcerated. Despite the fact that the father is dead and the mother is in prison, the DPW has failed thus far to determine the legal status of the children. It has not sought nor obtained custody of the children even though they were reported as having been abused by their only living parent who has since been convicted for child abuse.

Shortly after the DPW learned of the situation at the shelter, it acquiesced in an informal agreement of family friends to care for the children. Vickie went to live with Jim G. (Jay Sr.'s brother) and his wife, Jackie. Memphis went to live with childhood friends of Jay Sr., and Jay Jr. went to visit a paternal aunt in Florida and has never returned, nor has DPW conducted an investigation to determine whether his living situation is appropriate, or what his needs are.

Jay Sr.'s brother, as well as Jim and Jackie G., have not been screened, despite the fact that they live in Philadelphia, to determine whether they are appropriate foster parents or caretakers; nor have the childhood friends of Jay Sr., with whom Memphis is living.

In January 1990, Jackie G. advised DPW that her husband, Jim G. had physically abused Sherry. He suffers post-traumatic stress syndrome as a consequence of his participation in the Vietnam War. He receives counseling for this disorder once a month. According to the complainant, Jim picked Sherry up by her hair and hit her repeatedly in the face and head. Jackie subsequently obtained a restraining order against Jim, and sent Sherry and Vickie to live with her mother. The DPW failed to conduct an adequate and appropriate investigation of this abuse complaint, as required by law and reasonable professional standards.

Jackie was admitted several days later to the Northwest Institute for "severe depression," and under the circumstances she felt she could no longer care for the children. Sherry was admitted to the Department of Psychiatry at Eastern Pennsylvania Psychiatric Institute (EPPI) on January 13, 1990, as a means of protecting her from her threats of suicide and aggressive behavior, which included playing with a gas stove. The EPPI, in concluding its report on February 6, 1990, recommended that Sherry be placed in a residential care setting. Despite the recommendation, DPW did not place the child in residential care, nor did it make an appropriate determination in respect of whether it was safe for Sherry to return to Jim and Jackie. She was released into their care, with a promise that she would be placed in residential care shortly. As late as March 15, 1990, the placement had not occurred, nor had she received therapy or treatment. No one from the DPW has visited her since her return to the G's. Her mental state has continued to deteriorate. During the interim, DPW drafted a plan for Sherry, under which Jackie and Jim were requested to attend counseling sessions which instruct Jim to refrain from striking Sherry and pulling her hair. The plan further states that Sherry would be placed in residential care. However, as late as of July, 1990, no such placement had been identified ((*Neal et al. vs. Robert Casey et al.*, 1992, 28-32).

Two identical systemic weaknesses can be identified in the treatment of the girls in these cases; first, the scattering of siblings; and second, a nonchalance by DPW which ignores the welfare of a child, whom it "assumes" will be "all right." This is particularly so in respect to ensuring that the child receives the appropriate psychiatric treatment.

Marlene, unlike Memphis, it is hoped, was not sexually abused. However, the facts relating to this matter are not quite clear. The director refuses to make any comment on the situation as it existed in the foster home. Marlene, by her behavior, forced the termination of foster care. When questioned about this particular aspect of her stay in care, she simply responds by saying that she does not want to live with the couple as the wife has accused her of sleeping with her husband.

HAROLD

Harold is a 17-year-old. adolescent, whom the researcher met initially as a student in one of her emotional support classes. When the researcher first met Harold, he was failing most of his subjects. He had been placed in the special education class because it was believed that he was retarded, as well as having some behavioral problems. The researcher discovered on the first day of contact with Harold that he was not retarded at all; he was suffering from dyslexia. When the researcher read the text of a reading comprehension paper to him, he was able to answer all the questions correctly on each occasion.

(This experience is similar to that which the researcher had with another student in a MR class. This pretty honey-blond girl of approximately 11 years of age was both handicapped and categorized as mentally retarded. Because she had some difficulty in holding her pencil, during the period in which the other students in the class learned to write, she was left to her own devices. Seated in a special chair, she was allowed to look at magazines. The researcher having known her early childhood education teacher, who was well known for helping her students to achieve the highest possible goals, was astounded to find that this child was not writing. The researcher knew that if she had been in the former teacher's class, she had learned how to write some letters despite her handicap. Yet, throughout the year in this particular class, she had been allowed to languish. The researcher found a thick piece of chalk, which is easier to handle, took the child to the board, and wrote the letters "E, F, A, O I, L, and T," on the board and asked the child to copy the letters, using the thick chalk. The student copied the letters. The researcher then took a thick marker and a piece of paper and wrote the same letters, and asked the child to write them. The researcher then wrote the child's name alongside the letters which the student had written. At the bottom of the sheet, the researcher wrote the following message "These letters were written by your daughter, copying those which I wrote as an example. If she can do this, why is your child not writing in class everyday? Miss_____ , substitute teacher." The researcher has no idea what the reaction to this letter was, but certainly hopes that some action was taken. Here we have a situation in which there was obviously no follow up among special education teachers as to what the capacities of the students were.)

On the occasions when the researcher was in the emotional support class, Harold and his friend Jose were well behaved, studied and carried out their work without difficulty. However, on each occasion that the researcher was called to work in another classroom, the two students were either expelled or suspended. On one occasion, Harold entered the classroom and upon seeing the researcher said, to the other adults in charge," I was going to be bad today, but Miss _____ is here, so I'll be good." As a consequence, the researcher was perceived as not being "a team player" and was no longer requested for that class, on the grounds that after the researcher left the class, it took two to three weeks before those in charge could 'get students back to normal.' In general, the teachers' perceptions of students negated any progress a student could make. Upon arrival, they would make statements like, "Well, another day at the zoo."

Teacher attitudes play a significant role in the expectations and capacities of students to learn. Payne (1994), discusses the problem in the following manner:

> If teachers of LSES [lower socio-economic status] minority students, who are given ample opportunities for disparate attitudes and stereotypes to develop, hold firmly to the biases of the dominant culture, they are apt to misperceive their students' behavior and performance in all or some aspects. These misperceptions are likely to influence the educational system in terms of their effect on attribution acquisition, expectation formation, and motivation Bar Tal, 1979; Feldman & Saletsky; 1986; Graham, 1986; Weinstein, 1976). When these areas are weakened, teachers and their LSES minority students become increasingly alienated from each other. This alienation manifests itself in a negativism, isolation and powerlessness, and meaninglessness (182)
>
> Unfortunately, the educational system allows little opportunity for teachers to reflect on their attitudes, performance, or use of resources. Thus left to their own devices, some teachers may come to reject universalism, lower their goals, and/or discount some groups as unteachable (Buchman, 1986). (183)

Some months later, Harold was removed from the foster home in which he was staying at the time of attending special education classes and placed in the group home II, operated by the same organization for which the researcher had been working. According to his former foster parents, Harold had to be returned because the foster parents had left Harold at home and taken a weekend trip. Harold found the liquor in the liquor cabinet, invited his friends over, and hosted a large party during their absence. They found that this last act of disobedience, in combination with others (not mentioned), made it impossible to keep Harold in their home. The researcher believes that the above act is one in which any adolescent would participate if unsupervised for a weekend, if for no other reason than out of curiosity.

Harold's arrival at the group home II, was brought to the researcher's attention by a counselor at the residence, who quite by chance mentioned teaching to Harold, who in turn mentioned the name of a teacher whom he liked, who happened to be the researcher.

When the researcher learned that Harold was in the residence, she contacted the former foster parents in an effort to get the consent of the natural mother to visit Harold when he was on respite. The former foster parents contacted the agency, which upon finding out that the researcher had requested permission to see Harold, advised the foster parents to have no further contact with the researcher. When Harold was advised that the researcher had not been granted permission to visit, his behavior also began to deteriorate. This was prompted by several things. Harold wanted to be fostered by an African-American family. His main complaint to the researcher was that when he was fostered by a Caucasian family, they would not let him "be African-American." The researcher could readily understand this situation having spent many years in Australia. At the group home, a White, female counselor expressed the sentiment that she was "afraid" to be at the group home with Harold.

Harold was a very handsome, mixed-race boy, who was capable of presenting himself in an extremely well-behaved manner. He was soft spoken and intelligent and was not given to arguing. His main problem appeared to be that he was easily led and had a tendency to "act out." After three weeks under the supervision of the former inner city policeman, he too put his fist through the wall of one of the rooms at the residence after an argument, which took him beyond the point of his patience.

Harold was taken to the hospital for psychiatric assessment, but being a very intelligent individual, he refused to sign himself in and could not be kept. After this incident, the director decided that she would take Harold to the " Lifer's Program" (which was responsible for the production of the documentary *Scared Straight*.) Being fully aware of Harold's emotional condition, the researcher wrote to the executive director of the organization, requesting that he not allow Harold to attend that program as he was an adolescent who was already insecure and that such an experience might send him over the edge. The executive director ignored the researcher's request, and allowed the group home director to take Harold on the trip, which left him in a very unstable condition.

Upon learning that Harold was one of the researcher's former students in whom she took a great deal of interest, the organization attempted to get rid of Harold. It found him a job working at McDonald's, and shortly thereafter put him into an independent living program, under which he was responsible for paying his rent. Having received no instruction on budgeting, he soon found himself out of an apartment, being unable to pay his rent. Last seen, he was standing on a corner in a rural town of Monroe County, having nowhere to go and not knowing what to do.

ACLUF- Reflective Case Study II

ACLUF's reflective case in this instance is that of John B., who, like Sherry G., is an inner-city resident. John is a 14-year-old boy, whose parents in September, 1990 asked that he be placed in foster care. During his stay in care, John was frequently taunted by other residents in the group home where he lived. Despite his obvious history of neurological and psychological disorders, he did not receive psychiatric care. He ran away from the facility four times. Even though DHS was aware of his unhappiness, no effort was made to find a more appropriate placement for him. The last time John ran away, he went to live with a friend. DHS made no effort to find him for several weeks, never visited the friend's home and made no arrangements for John to attend school during the several weeks he was away. John was eventually returned to the care of his natural parents. However, no psychiatric treatment was provided (*Neal et al Baby. vs. Robert Casey et al.*, 1992, 157-159).

In the two cases given above, the reader will note that once the adolescents left the facility no further follow up took place. Both boys were left to their own devices. Neither Harold, nor John B.'s education appears to have been a serious concern of the agencies.

At the time Harold arrived at group home II, he had been mainstreamed at high school; however, nothing had been done about his apparent dyslexia. Harold's obviously delicate emotional condition was not taken into consideration before forcing him to attend the "Lifer's Program." The brashness with which the visitors are treated works well for 'street punks," but Harold was not in this category. He had obviously at one time been in the care of someone who taught him all the social graces required to succeed in life. His misbehavior was more a situation of "acting out" both as a means of relieving the boredom he experienced in the special education class and as an attempt to obtain peer approval. After his experience with the "Lifer's Program," he was shaken and said to one of his counselors, "Now I have even less esteem than I had before."

As for John, he is afraid that his parents will return him to foster care. After his return, his caseworker did not visit him, nor did the caseworker ensure that he was enrolled in therapy. From the foregoing it will be appreciated that the service and the responsibilities of the child protective services have not been carried out at an effective level. The failure to provide the requisite service to youth in need today will have a significant impact on the stature of tomorrow's citizens. The negative outcomes of children in care will impact the United States' future citizenry by producing a generation of illiterate and irresponsible adults.

James P. Comer, a Professor at Yale Medical School's Child Study Center, said during an interview with Nick Chiles (1993) that:

Unless we educate all the children, in 30 years and certainly in
60 years, we're going to be a Third World country because we
won't be able to compete; we won't have enough well-educated
people. But America doesn't see that; it wants to see the here

and now. That kind of narrowness and selfishness has gotten the country in trouble and continues to take it on a downhill course. (86)

As will be appreciated from the foregoing, there is a good deal of discrepancy between what state and federal government statutes perceive as adequate care for state wards, and conditions as they actually exist. The researcher found that, with respect to regulations pertaining to the services provided to foster parents and those actually in force, there was a good deal of discrepancy.

FOSTER CARE: THE FOSTER PARENTS' PERSPECTIVES

Before proceeding with an examination of the researcher's findings, the researcher would like to focus on the area of treatment foster services, as support for her contention that foster parents are under-paid, and under-serviced. This is particularly important because one of the families interviewed by the researcher was also in the treatment foster care program. Treatment foster service is an expanding area in out-of-home care. It is provided to children under the child protective services who have serious emotional, behavioral, or medical problems.

A study conducted by Meadowcroft, Thomlison, & Chamberlain (1994) reveals that the system is less expensive when compared to residential services (i.e., group homes, or institutionalization). It is also perceived as more favorable from the behavioral development perspective of the youth in care because it provides a less restrictive environment (566). The program recruits foster parents specifically to work with severely challenged (mentally or physically fragile) children. According to Meadowcroft et al. (1994), foster treatment parents are paid at higher rates than foster parents involved with ostensibly normal children. They function as professional members of a treatment team and provide care in their own homes to the clients. Foster treatment parents receive an initial 18 hours of training before they receive a child with severe emotional problems, and an additional 20 hours of in-service training thereafter. The parents are responsible for only one child, and provide care on a one-to-one basis for an average period of 15 months. Payment to foster parents involved in this type of work ranges from $27.00 to $35.00 per day (569). Meadowcroft et al. state that studies conducted by Osmand (1992) and Thomlison and Unrau (1993) revealed:

> These authors found no empirical support for differentiating the types of activities that treatment parents did from those that foster parents did; rather, the difference appeared to lie in the intensity and frequency required of these activities. Both treatment parents and traditional foster parents reported satisfaction in working with children placed in their homes, but traditional foster parents were more dissatisfied with the lack of worker contact, lack of planning for the child, and lack of regard for their viewpoints. (571)

The average payment made to foster parents not under the foster treatment parents program in rural Pennsylvania is approximately $17.00 per day, as was revealed through the interviews the researcher had with foster parents.

The researcher will now continue with an examination of situations surrounding the question of foster care as it affects the foster parent/child relationship. The researcher circulated questionnaires to minority foster parents in Monroe County. The minority population fostering youth in this area continues to be extremely small. The paucity of minority foster parents presents a serious problem to the psychological welfare of minority youths in care. The problem becomes even more significant for those in care who have reached adolescence and have had an opportunity to know and assimilate their culture, before coming into care. These youths are particularly handicapped when placed in foster or group home care where the parent is a non-minority, or where there are very few minority counselors.

The questionnaire distributed to minority foster parents (Appendix D) focused on four areas:

1. The educational background, age of foster parent and experience working with children.

2. The foster child (number of children fostered, developmental age as compared to chronological age, age of children in care, sex, race, racial awareness, period of fostering and any behavior which exhibited signs of attachment/unattachment, and conduct disorder.)

3. Agency relationship (caseworker, supplying parents' need for respite, funds for unexpected needs, training, foster parent/natural parent contact.)

4. The foster care relationship (length, number of children, period of care, reason for termination, if relationship was terminated.)

The researcher, in response to item one, inquired as to the professional status of each foster family and found that their qualifications were well suited to the needs of children in care. In respect of age, the parents ranged in age from approximately the early 40s to late 50s. They were teachers, psychologists, accountants, and there was one practical nurse. All of the parents had raised children of their own. It would appear therefore that with respect to the screening process as it relates to minority foster parents, selection is carried out very efficiently to ensure all foster parents meet the criteria required. Additional stipulations made by both the private agencies and C & Y are that at least one foster parent must hold a full-time job, and that no more than six children can be taken into care at one time (Foster treatment care parents are allowed only one child.)

Inquiries and responses made by parents in respect of item two above, revealed the following:

1. Boys are more likely to be selected over girls for fostering.

2. There is a strong preference for younger children.

3. Children are more likely to be returned upon reaching late childhood/pre-adolescence.

In respect of one above, the number of boys selected over girls appeared to indicate a sexual preference for boys, but could also be related to the higher incidence of males in the system. However, in foster homes in which two foster parents were present, there was a preference for boys. All the foster parents interviewed expressed a strong disinclination toward opening their homes to girls and, more specifically, adolescent girls. Reasons for this ranged from fear of teenage pregnancy, to allegations of sexual abuse and rape. The findings therefore indicated that teenage girls were least likely to be welcomed in a foster home in the area. However, it came to the researcher's attention that licensed, foster treatment parents did take female adolescents for short periods, while awaiting placement of the girl in the home of a relative or a group home. The general inclination was, however, away from adolescent girls.

There was a distinct preference for infants and toddlers, because it was hoped that they could more easily be directed and properly trained. Also it was hoped that they had not as yet become unattached. Magid and McKelvey (1987) say of this situation:

> Infants and toddlers have much faster "internal clocks" than adults do. You just can't make an infant wait too long to begin the attachment process. If you do, it may never happen. The tragedy of the present adoption and foster-care system is that it often makes children wait, in limbo, before trying to settle them into a new home.
>
> To prevent such breaks from occurring in children already at risk, a total revamping of the child adoption and foster care industry is needed. Hundreds of thousands of children have been injured, perhaps permanently through bureaucratic delays and bungling caused by the current system. unwittingly, delays in permanent placement of adoptive children are causing them to become unattached. Some critics even say delays are not caused by bureaucracy gone astray, but by profit seekers. They charge that foster care is more profitable than permanent adoption so children are therefore kept in temporary homes. (148)

Younger girls were more likely to be accepted in single-headed households where the foster parent was female. Young girls (usually infants two years and under) were more likely to be fostered by parents who were taking siblings. This was done with a view to keeping siblings together as much as possible. However, the findings of the interview and questionnaire, as well as observations made by the researcher of African-American and non-African-American foster parents fostering minority children, was that the chances of being fostered in a home environment was significantly decreased if the client was an adolescent and female. This is an area which certainly deserves a great deal more research, particularly in view of the fact that these adolescent females are going to be the mothers of future US citizens.

The interviews and questionnaires also revealed that children were more likely to be returned into protective services' care upon reaching late childhood and early adolescence. The reason given for this was that at this age, children began to display conduct disorder-related behavior. This took the form of wanton destruction of property—both the child's and that of the foster parents (i.e., defacing property, destroying household furniture, disobeying, lack of respect, willfulness, sexual explicitness, such as reading or purchasing adult rated materials, running away, poor behavior at school, theft and lying). (See table at Appendix E.)

Of the families interviewed, foster families "A" and "C" had taken adolescents into their homes for a short period. In the first instance, foster family "C" had taken and returned a 13 year old girl. She had tried to commit suicide and blamed the attempt, when caught, as being a means of relieving her anxiety over having been sexually assaulted by an older son of the fostering family, who generally did not live at the home. The truth was revealed. The accused was no where near the area claimed to be the site of the rape at the time and date alleged.

Foster family "A" returned a 17-year-old. boy because he ran away repeatedly and also slipped out of the house at night to join peers in car theft-related activities. Additionally, the youth was destructive, sexually active, and careless about the number and types of women with whom he had contact.

When questioned, foster parents "A" and "C" gave two reasons for giving up the children. These two reasons were more important than the behavior of the foster child to them. The first was that the agency was inclined to believe the youth as opposed to the foster parent. This situation created a very negative attitude toward the caseworker by the foster parent. In many instances, the foster parents were equally agitated by the fact that caseworkers were too young. Many had no children of their own and lacked real life experience, hence the advice they gave to the foster parents reflected this inexperience, and could not be taken as counseling which was beneficial. The visits made by caseworkers were deemed to be an obvious waste of time.

Second, all foster parents felt personally responsible for the behavior of the youth in their care. They believed inappropriate behavior directly reflected on their parenting skills, despite the fact that they were aware that many children in foster care do have psychological problems. An additional reason for giving up the children was that some foster children went out of their way to annoy neighbors (i.e., injuring neighborhood pets, defacing property, and ostracizing neighbors). Foster parents perceived behavior of this type as threatening their acceptance in the neighborhood, particularly when considering their minority status and that of the foster child.

The researcher also sought to discover through the use of the questionnaire, whether younger children had begun to exhibit behavior related to unattachment. According to the responses, even newborn infants displayed stiffening when being caressed or kissed. Older infants and very young children, (the total number of children taken by the families interviewed was 10, ranging in age from newborn to 17 years) also displayed a lack of congruence between their chronological and mental ages. This manifested itself in a lack of general knowledge specific to children at certain stages of development. Foster family "C" had a child of approximately three years, who was unable upon arrival at the foster home, to correctly identify and distinguish between a cat and a horse. Other foster children taken by the same family exhibited behavior considered inappropriate for their chronological age.

In the case of foster family "A," their first foster child, who was an eight-year- old, still used language equivalent to that of an infant aged two years. He would say things like "me want water," or express himself in broken English, "Is you mad at me?" despite the fact that the child had been living with a Caucasian family for a number of years. This child, like many others was unaware of his own racial background and culture and had to be reoriented in terms of his racial history and cultural identity.

By age 10, his behavior had begun to deteriorate to the extent that the foster mother, who was an early education teacher, was unable to care for him, having recently survived a severe physical illness. The boy was returned to the agency, which told her that he was being fostered by another professional African-American couple. After some investigation into the matter, the foster parents discovered that the boy had been given to two Caucasian homosexual males. The obvious intentional misinformation given to the relinquishing foster parents is just the first item in a pandora's box of systemic inconsistencies, half truths, and cover ups.

The Drake study (1994) which was conducted with a view to obtaining worker and client views of competencies in the child welfare services, found that "Worker honesty is an essential competency, according to these clients. Several clients were quite bitter when workers provided them with inaccurate, or false information." (598)

The study identifies key worker-client relationship competencies which are necessary to ensure an efficient and effective relationship between the client and service providers (see Table at Appendix F).

Of the three families interviewed, all complained of inadequate funds to meet the needs of the children. One parent, upon arriving at the agency to collect an infant, was given the baby wrapped in a blanket. There accompanied no crib, diapers, clothing of any type, bassinet, carriage, bottles, baby tub, or necessities for infant care. The foster mother was told to provide these and reimbursement would be made later. This created a particularly inconvenient situation for the foster parent, who did not have the funds to make such large expenditures.

In the instance of foster family "B," they received a young boy who had been staying with an Amish family. His clothing was so tight it barely covered his body and at one point the new foster mother thought she would have to cut the clothes from his body in order to remove them. He had been poorly cared for, was unaware of his racial background, had obviously never been exposed to other African-Americans and, as a consequence, was afraid of them. Despite his age of 14 months, he made no attempt to speak, but instead screamed constantly. Screaming was the only form of communication he employed and he screamed for whatever he wanted. He was in poor physical condition, lacked iron, and had skin problems.

Agency relationships with foster parents vary. Some parents boasted of having an excellent relationship with the agency and the caseworker; for others, it was nothing less than a nightmare. Such conditions can prevail within the same agency, as has been illustrated by the foster parent interviews. Some of the families had taken children from the same agencies. All agencies were in Pennsylvania. All agencies drew their children from inner city areas. Foster family "B" reported having an excellent relationship with the caseworker and the agency itself. The agency provided funding for visits to the natural mother by the foster children at least once a month, during which the foster mother was able to keep the natural mother appraised of the children's progress. The other two families had relationships which were very bad and experienced, among other things, lack of support in respect of the period during which the children were giving them the most trouble. All of the families interviewed complained about at least one, if not all, of the following conditions:

1. untimely payment of foster care fees
2. unable to contact agency in an emergency
3. difficulty in obtaining reimbursement for out of pocket expenses related to child care
4. agency was slow in providing respite assistance
5. agency requested services and expenditures beyond those deemed to be the responsibility of the foster parent (i.e. use of personal car to drive long distances for health care, family visits, etc., without mileage reimbursement)
6. poor caseworker/foster parent relationship
7. poor caseworker/foster child relationship (In one instance the caseworker was so slow in delivering the foster child's Christmas presents from the agency, they were still in the back of her car in May when she came to get him for reassignment.)
8. agency does not provide adequate funding for child's clothing and other needs
9. foster parents are poorly paid
10. because children are on Medicare, specialists, doctors and health facilities are always far away from the town in which the children live
11. caseworker attitudes toward the manner in which the foster parent is managing the child's daily life
12. lack of candidness about child's previous placements, psychological profile, intellectual capacity and psychological profiles and histories of the parents are not provided.

FOSTER CARE:
EXAMINING AGENCY RESPONSIBILITY AND
ORGANIZATIONAL STRUCTURE

The researcher then reviewed the promises made by organizations to prospective foster parents and contributors, by examining foster parent publications supplied by the agencies and annual reports, when possible. The first of the organizations, in addressing prospective foster parents, touted its many years of service to the area's children.

Espoused also was the philosophy that in dealing with behaviorally at risk youth and those with severe emotional problems, it took the approach of "Reality Therapy." Reality Therapy emphasizes the responsibility of the individual for his or her own behavior. It stresses the individual's strengths and abilities to make choices and changes in his/her life—to take control over life's direction. The organization responded in the brochure to the question, "What do I need to learn to become a foster parent?," with "No previous parental experience is necessary, but it can be very helpful." Responding to the question "Where do these foster children come from?," it answered, "These children generally come from abuse situations and/or long-term patterns of neglect."

The organization also runs concurrently an intensive foster care program, which is another term used to describe foster treatment care, which the reader will recall is designed for children who are severely emotionally disturbed. Yet no previous parental experience is required. In most instances the foster parent will only receive up to 18 hours of training before the child enters the home.

The second agency, which is by far the largest, contracts children to the smaller organizations. It also provides services to a large number of children with emotional and behavioral difficulties and runs concurrently 27 other services. As well, it operates treatment facilities in 25 locations in five states. According to its brochure, from its commencement to the present, it has assisted over 15,000 youths.

This organization is not a non-profit undertaking, in that it charges for services, but does claim that 93% of earned revenue goes directly back to the children. The organization refused to provide the researcher with an annual report, stating that the organization did not publish one.

The organization has among its national directors some very well known individuals who are influential and connected with the more esteemed Ivy League universities in the US. Foster parent "C," who was given the baby with no accompanying provisions, was contracted to care for foster children with this agency. Also, the researcher phoned their offices one day, seeking to volunteer and was told, "Why don't you go out and help some nice children, like those in the girl scouts?"

The organization's foster parent recruitment material states that respite is provided for the foster parent by persons who are fully approved. But, it was the foster parent "C's" experience, that the agency did not act responsibly in assisting with matters concerned with the care of the child when it was most needed, and in providing funds to cover unanticipated expenses.

In matters concerned with training, it would appear that the agency has a significantly longer period of training than others—two years. Training is provided to families in various settings with a view to meeting the families' needs for convenience. The organization also provides liability insurance for families while the children are in placement. This insurance, however, is only supplemental to the foster parents' own insurance policy. Therefore, in the event of a fire-setting incident which caused the loss of the family home, the organization would not be responsible for the full cost of the loss. Fire setting is one of the major maladaptive behaviors of conduct disordered children. It is quite understandable that the agency would be somewhat cautious in this regard; however, the foster parent is left with the onus of the financial burden.

As in the case of the larger agencies, it was revealed during the study that smaller organizations also were greatly diversified for size. It could be reasoned that this might be a significant cause of the failure of smaller agencies to provide efficient and effective service. Diversification has always been considered by not-for-profit organizations to be a safeguard which will increase the likelihood of the perpetuation of the organization.

However, the tactic has changed with respect to the provision of service. Unlike the March of Dimes, which for many years concentrated on the eradication of polio and then later on birth defects, once a vaccine was found for polio, the newer organizations tend to diversify before the immediate goals have been achieved. For example, a smaller, well-known private agency in rural Pennsylvania is burdened with trying to effectively meet the demands of eight programs, which it runs concurrently. These span a spectrum of services which encompass the provision of transient shelter for runaways; family unification (adolescents with families); an adolescent life skills program; family preservation (to prevent the placement of children in out-of-home care); a drug prevention program; a child abuse program; and a family therapeutic foster care program (group homes). As will be appreciated, some of these programs replicate the services provided by others under the same organizational umbrella. Additionally, many go beyond the province of the area of care, as in the case of the drug abuse prevention program. Upon examining the programs conducted by the larger organization, one finds that despite the large number of programs provided, they are properly designed to meet the areas of psychological needs of the youth in care and do not expand into services outside the province of its expertise.

It has been the researcher's experience in examining various organizations outside the area under study, that drug and alcohol rehabilitation, usually is a field that requires total concentration of energies in the specific area of rehabilitation and that organizations working on this specific problem do not move into the area of runaway shelters, or other tenuously related services Therefore it could be surmised that the focus of this smaller agency is too expansive.

Despite the wide range of services provided, only 2,500 clients were served during 1993. According to the graph provided at the back of its annual report, the largest number of clients served were under the drug and alcohol program. The figure provided for this was nearly 900 clients. The next largest consumer of services was the adolescents and families together program for which services were provided to approximately 700 clients. The transient shelter for runaways consumed the third largest amount of services, ranging between 400 and 500 clients. From that point there was a significant decline in the number of clients served, which would bring into question the necessity of providing these services at all—particularly as they replicate services provided by other human services organizations in the area. Since the services receiving the most clients were drug and rehabilitation and family reunification, it might be more feasible to focus on drug and rehabilitation with a view to family reunification

Does the organization live up to its stated goals? In its annual report it states that its goal for the adolescent life skills program is to assist adolescent participants in their effort to (a) complete their education, (b) get and keep a job, (c) find an apartment, (d) learn budgeting, and (e) develop skills needed to live independently. This is the same organization which had Harold and Marlene in its care.

The majority of new case referrals to this organization come from schools (46%). There is a sharp decline at that point to 14% which come from families and C & Y; other private agencies provide only 5% of referral sources; the police 4%; juvenile probation 3%; friends 2%; and the organization through its own resources approximately 7%. Of the $2,436, 000 in total revenue received for the 1993-94 fiscal year, the organization spent $1,318,463 in salaries and wages, which were necessary to the operation of the eight programs. Approximately half of its clients are minorities (African-American, Latino and other), yet the number of minority workers is far below the acceptable standard—particularly in Monroe County.

Turning to the question of the candidness of agencies providing information to prospective foster parents, this aspect was one that was seen as a significant problem for two of the three families interviewed. The family "A" expressed the following sentiments in discussing its agency:

> The agency was definitely not truthful about information regarding background and on one child there was absolutely no social history. The worker said, "We like to keep that in the office." I didn't really know where he came from and where he had been (in terms of early development and family information).

When asked about the relationship with the caseworker and administrative staff, this family responded, "The relationship was superficial. Appointments were kept approximately 25% of the time. [This is in regard to one agency]. It was felt that the caseworker never really knew the child." Family "A" reported not having seen any minority professionals which were affiliated with this organization.

In the case of family, "B" the children were so young that case history was almost totally irrelevant. The agency to which they are contracted does, however, arrange for two of the three children in care to meet with their parents and arranges foster parent/parent visits. The family has had a very supportive relationship with the caseworker, who has tried to satisfy all the needs of the fostering family. The agency with which this foster family is working is located closer to Philadelphia, and the family reports that it has on many occasions seen minority members who were affiliated with the agency in a professional capacity.

Family "C" reported very poor agency/parent relationships in all of the agencies it had worked with. These agencies served the Monroe County area. The foster family also reported not having seen any minority members in professional positions in these agencies. The foster children who were old enough to attend school, had all been placed in special education classes.

THE CONDITION OF FOSTER YOUTHS AT SCHOOL AND THE QUESTION OF AGENCY/SCHOOL COOPERATION

The researcher begins this section of the study with her observations of the condition of foster youths in special education classes, and with the observation that foster families reported that in none of the schools attended by their wards were there minority teachers. Monroe County has one African-American principal and three or four teachers out of the total teaching population in all of its elementary, middle, and high schools. The researcher, who taught special education as a substitute teacher in a number of these schools, was astounded to find that whenever she entered a school, the minority students nudged one another to direct attention to the unusual sight of a African-American teacher in a Monroe County school. The students in grades, 1-3, 5-8, and 9-12, for purposes of clarity, will be categorized as "A," "B," and "C."

The primary observation was that many foster children in group "A," come to school hungry. As a remedy for this situation, many special education teachers provide food at their own expense. When asked why they had done so, they generally responded in these terms. "I can't teach them if they're hungry because they can't pay attention. Some of them have no regular bed time, so they get up late and leave the house without eating." However, upon questioning the children in category "A," the researcher found, particularly in cross-racial foster situations, that the children did not like the food. Two questions immediately arise in this respect:

1. Is the food prepared at home different from that to which the children were accustomed?
2. Are the foster parents providing enough discipline, or are the children generally left to their own devices on important matters of this type?

Students in the group "B" category also experienced hunger and many of the teachers working with students in these grades also provided snacks at their own expense. It was observed, however, that unlike the children in the early grades, hunger was experienced by both White and African-American students. Though many of these students were fostered, others at risk of hunger were with their families. If cutbacks in the school lunch program occur, many children may experience severe malnutrition, as the school lunch and/or breakfast programs represent the only significant meal/meals they get during a 24-hour period. Student hunger among both foster and children at home requires further research to determine the numbers and the severity, and what the child protective services is doing about this problem.

Few students at group "C" level complained of hunger, but the researcher noted that the main reinforcement employed to assure continued good behavior was food. Different types of snacks were designated for the performance of specific tasks, in some emotionally handicapped classrooms in which students ranged in age from 15 to 20. For example, a candy bar would provide the teacher with a student who was willing to clean up the classroom (i.e., pick up dropped papers from the floor, arrange the desks in proper order, and put away books and writing implements which had been left out after the last period). This type of inducement would have had very little effect if the children were not hungry, or had the means to purchase their own snacks.

The researcher concluded from the above observations that one of the factors contributing to the difficulty of teaching students in special education is hunger. While it is very gracious of teachers to provide food for such children, the researcher contends that instances of child hunger should be reported to the appropriate authorities. This may well have been the case, but no teacher was willing to discuss the matter further.

The second factor which has a negative impact on the abilities of teachers to work with foster and special education students in the classroom is that of teacher-to-teacher communication. With respect to group "A" classes, there is a greater likelihood of agency/educational institution liaison, but the transmittal of information regarding the psychological condition of children in care appears to diminish at two levels: (a) within the same classroom, at teacher-to-teacher level; and (b) between special education teacher-to-mainstream teacher.

At the teacher-to-teacher level within the same classroom, Haring and Phillips (1967) perceive the necessity of transferring information as crucial to the welfare of the children in class; and have the following to say:

> The teaching assistant with a background of regular presence can often lessen or even preclude the disruption of class routine. For these reasons the assistant teacher needs to be included in the training of teachers for such special classes; a pinch hitter needs to know the rules of the games just as much as the regular team member. (122)

In most instances teacher-to-teacher communication within the classroom environment is fragmented. Early education teachers are in the best position to obtain information from the agency as part of the intake process. Teachers working at level "A" often have one or two assistants, depending on the number of children in the classroom. It is in the classroom environment at teacher-to-teacher level that communication can break down, since the acquisition of information relating to specific students by teacher aides is contingent upon the teacher's willingness to share such information. During staff/administration/foster parent meetings which are set for the purpose of examining Individual Education Plans (IEPs) with a view to revising existing goals upward or downward, it is normally the practice for the special education teacher to attend without the aide. However, it is often the aide who is more intimately involved with the student throughout the day. It is assumed by those attending the meeting, and the agency, that information pertaining to factors which impact the child's behavior, or capacity to learn will be transmitted by the teacher to the assistants. This does not always occur. Additionally, previous poor experiences with the agencies can also result in the failure of the teacher to inquire from the agency or transmit information further. Teachers have learned to be wary of social service involvement, which can often be frustrating and fruitless. This pervading sense of powerlessness is often shared by the principal (Fennimore, 1989, 128-130), and the teacher is left feeling that it is better for all teaching staff to work with students at a more superficial level, as opposed to becoming involved with the student's welfare at agency level.

It was the researcher's experience that most special education teachers in group "A" were at least adequately informed about the foster children in their classes. However, in depth knowledge of student behavior was more often supplied by the foster parent as a consequence of experience, than by the agency. The teachers who were most at risk of experiencing unpredictable/uncontrollable behavior and who were least prepared to handle such situations were the mainstream teachers.

The latest trend in special education is toward mainstreaming. This experimental method of education is being undertaken not only with mentally challenged students, but also with those who have been classified as having behavioral problems. Students in this category are allowed to attend a number of mainstream classes. This attendance is contingent upon their ability to adjust their behavior. The attendance of special education foster children in mainstream classes can often present a problem for mainstream teachers because they are not usually advised of specific problems which may arise because of the special family problems which have negatively impacted the lives of these children. In an effort to provide some indication of the problem, the researcher selected a number of mainstream teachers who are also categorized under the same "A," "B," "C" grade levels as those given for the special education teachers. They were given the identical questionnaire as special education teachers (Appendix G). This measure was taken to discover how well the agency and/or special education teachers liaised with mainstream teachers at levels "B" and "C," accepting special education foster care students. The questionnaire made inquiry into:

1. whether teachers had been aware of the presence of foster children in their classes; and if they presented a problem
2. whether they were invited to attend IEP meetings, or had agency or social worker contact with those responsible for the education and welfare of the foster child
3. they were also requested to provide suggestions as to what could be done to facilitate the teaching of students in this category.

The majority of mainstream teachers stated that they had at least one minority foster student in their classroom. All indicated that they had not been advised by the agency that the child would be in their class, nor had any IEP meetings been arranged with them between themselves and the agency. The agencies have a policy of keeping confidential, details about their clients. It is assumed that mainstream teachers, if necessary, would be briefed by the school as to the exceptionalities of special education foster children. This was not happening. This attitude confirms earlier statements made by the ACLUF and the researcher that much of onus for follow up in respect of education and the general welfare is presumed by the agency to be something that will be handled by others.

When asked for suggestions as to what the mainstream teachers felt would be of assistance to them in facilitating the education of these students, they responded with the need to first, notify the teacher before the student arrives in the classroom. Information on the areas of sensitivity and/or special needs of the student would be useful. Second, they should be provided with information pertaining to the background and history of the student.

What are some of the past experiences of minority foster care students which could make them difficult to teach? The following excerpt taken from Madeline Cartwright's book *For the Children,* (1993) presents a full and realistic view of the lives of children living in inner city areas today:

For the past twenty years there has been a steady, concerted, almost conscious desertion of the principles and the programs that were at the heart of the civil rights movement of the 1950s and 1960s. The poor and the dispossessed minorities and white alike, have been virtually forsaken by a government answerable almost exclusively to the interests of the privileged.

Much press has been given to the murder and chaos in our cities, but relatively few spotlights have been aimed at the schools. Oh, it happens. A newspaper or magazine reporter might venture in and write a story maybe about something heartwarming, even inspiring. A television crew might follow with its cameras. A radio team may arrive armed with tapes and microphones.

But when the reporters leave, middle America might mull over the stories over coffee. But nothing is done. Who has the time? Who has the money? who has the plan?

Meanwhile, many children live in homes where they must feed and care for one another because their parents are away from home. For too many children, whose "home" is no more than a corner of a condemned building where they tear the boards off the windows, light a kerosene heater for warmth and fetch water in empty plastic soda bottles, life goes on.

For too many of them, living moment to moment with the reality of death on their doorsteps, with bodies—drunken or dead—littering their path to school, life goes on.

What does homework mean to an eight-year-old boy who has nursed his mother through an overdose the night before.

What does the threat of suspension mean to a ten-year-old girl who is selling herself on the street and is more at home there than she is anywhere else in her life?

What does discipline mean to a boy or girl who has been behind bars and found that situation better than home or the neighborhood? What does the "future" mean to a child who wonders if he will live to or beyond the age of twenty-five? (6 -7)

It will be appreciated from the foregoing that the world from which these children emerge when they attend school is quite different from that of middle-class America, White or African-American. The realities which accost their daily lives, of course, have an impact on their perceptions, realities, and understandings.

With a view to pressing the point home, the researcher refers to Jane M. Healy's *Endangered Minds (1990)*. In it, she discusses neural plasticity of the brain and a discussion, which she held with Dr. Marian Diamond. Dr. Diamond, who is a professor of neuroanatomy at the University of California at Berkeley, had the following to say about the impact of the environment on the structure of the brain:

> Heredity plays a highly important role in the form of these different [behavioral] repertoires, but we now have clear evidence that the environment can play a role in shaping brain structure and, in turn learning behavior. It is the area of the brain that is stimulated that grows.
>
> To those of us in the field, there is absolutely no doubt that culture changes brains, and there's no doubt in my mind that children's brains are changing. . . . Whatever they're learning, as those nerve cells are getting input, they are sending out dendritic branches. As long as stimuli come in to a certain area, you get more branching; if you lose the stimuli, they stop branching. It is the pattern of the branching that differentiates among us. The cortex is changing all the time. (48-49)

These findings are frightening when one considers what is taking place within the environments of youth presently in care.

Despite this severe disadvantage, most poor minority children begin their first years of school with as much enthusiasm as students in any other economic bracket. However, the enthusiasm wanes as they become aware of the fact that the curriculum, as well as the perceptions of their teachers, differ from theirs. Alton D. Rison provides a pictograph at Appendix H which gives some insight into the type of forces arrayed against the minority student in his/her battle to achieve goals associated with success by middle-class America.

Having taken note of the above factors which impact the personalities, lifestyles, and perceptions of students in special education who are also in foster care, the researcher then circulated questionnaires to special education teachers. The reader will recall that it was the researcher's contention, that of the three categories of special education teachers, those in category "A" would be most likely to be in a position to liaise with the agency because of the necessity of drafting preliminary IEPs. The responses to the question revealed a totally different finding. Special education teachers were given the seven question document with a view to discovering the following:

1. The type and extent of agency/teacher contact.
2. The extent of information provided to teachers in special education with respect to any problems the student has which might make instruction in a classroom environment difficult for the teacher.
3. Suggestions which would facilitate the teaching of students in this category.

The responses given to answers by all categories of teachers were nearly identical. This included the questionnaires circulated to teachers from other states also. Teachers in each category had foster children in their classes and had not been notified by the agencies of their specific status. The majority of children were minorities and in most cases the teachers found the children difficult to handle. In some instances one foster student was well behaved and another poorly behaved, but all teachers agreed that they were more difficult to teach because of their behavior.

When asked whether they had been advised by a caseworker or anyone from the agency as to the behavioral problems they might encounter, they responded with a unanimous "NO!" In addition to the difficulty of the situation presented by not knowing anything about the background of the student, most special education teachers were confronted with having to draft an IEP for each student. Teachers said that most of the information they received about the student came from the foster parent. However, the foster parent was not in a position to provide the teacher with a psychological assessment of the child, nor, in most instances, could the foster parent provide any information about the child's history.

Not one of the special education teachers reported having met with the caseworkers of the foster care students. The similarity in response to that of mainstream teachers was so close, that the researcher perceived no difference in the situation of either group.

V

Summary, Conclusions and Recommendations

FOSTER CARE

How do Present Foster Care Arrangements Contribute to Social Disaffection in Minority Youth?

Based on the data contained in the questionnaires and the foster parents' responses during interview, the researcher found that there is a preference for fostering adolescent males, as opposed to females. This preference may well produce some very serious consequences in terms of the capacity of young women in foster care to form positive attachments. The seriousness of the situation should be considered in light of its potential to negatively impact future mother/child relationships when these girls are old enough to become mothers.

McWhirter (1993) states that approximately 1.1 million girls become pregnant each year in the United States. This means that approximately 3,000 teenage girls become pregnant every day. Of these 2,300 do so through error. Nearly half (550,000) carry the pregnancy to full term. Girls under the age of 15 represent 125,000 of the total figure given. Nineteen percent (19%) of these pregnancies will represent second births and 33% repeat pregnancies. In other words, 20% of the female population will become pregnant before the age of 18 (20% White and 40% African-American). (138) (See Figure at Appendix I.) If these girls have not received the nurturing and guidance necessary to help them to take on the role of mothering, the consequence could be either abusive parenting, or a significant increase in children placed in out-of-home care, due to the mothers' lack of parenting skills and ability to bond.

Massat (1995) undertook a study to investigate the question of parent age and its relationship to maltreatment. She found that adolescent parents did not figure significantly in abuse reports. However, as mentioned earlier, there has been a growing trend in the number of children being cared for by older relatives, in homes where the natural parent does not reside. This factor would have a significant impact on Massat's finding. The researcher believes a follow-up study may well be warranted in about five years, when the burgeoning numbers of children under 12 in out-of-home care reach adolescence and become physically capable of parenthood. At that time, researchers may be better able to appreciate any disaffection/parental unattachment which could result from the lack of nurturing within a family atmosphere, or within a good foster/adoptive home, at present.

The number of reassignments of both males and females are additional factors, which increase the likelihood of instability in the youth in care. In many cases, youths are taken from a foster home environment, and placed in a group home environment, then taken out of a group home environment and placed in a foster home environment. The shifting back and forth is extremely difficult to adapt to, not only in terms of the accommodation environment, but also in terms of domestic structure and anticipated behavior. While the first requires the youth to behave as a family member, the latter, is structured almost regimentally, in terms of times to eat, bathe, look at television, etc. The continual bouncing back and forth between these two environments is probably more psychologically destabilizing than moving from foster home to foster home.

Another major cause of disaffection in minority youths in care, is related to the relationship which the group homes have with the rest of the community. The shelter which group homes provide is carried out in isolation to the rest of the community. In other words, despite the fact that the group home is located within the community, it is not part of the community. In the majority of cases, the home is not wanted in the community. A situation like this can have a very negative effect on the youths' ability to function within a community as active and caring members. This is particularly so if, additional to this problem, the residents' ethnicity is different to that of the community in which the group home is located.

The negative impact on the individual who is denied the opportunity of interpersonal contact is obvious. In this regard, this study has noted that even babies under a year old, can manifest unattachment. In the instance of very young children taken in foster care, a significant factor contributing to the existence of this behavior is the lapse of time between the infant's certification of good health at the hospital and its arrival at an appropriate home. Early signs of unattachment are stiffening when caressed, pushing away from any demonstration of affection and crankiness on being held. In older infants (1-3 years), antisocial behavior and unattachment can take the form of failure to speak, as in the case of the foster parent "B's" child who screamed for everything.

The failure of the system to properly and quickly match parents to children has been seen as a failure on the part of the management information services to provide data on available homes. Excessive periods of delay in providing information on the availability of adoptive parents and the inability to ensure expeditious permanent placement of an infant held in care, can prove psychologically detrimental.

Magid & McKelvey (1987, 148) contend that the failure of the child protective services to provide homes in a timely manner, has its basis in greed. According to the researchers, funding to organizations is higher if children are kept in temporary homes, than when provided with a permanent adoption situation.

There are also critical stages of development during which instability is extremely harmful. Pre-adolescence (10-12 years) is a stage of development during which the child is extremely impressionable. This is particularly so, because for the first time in the child's development, it begins to understand time in terms of past and present. The child is now able to use this time as a framework for his/her experience, and the two as a premise for possible future events. For example, at this age it is possible for a child to say, "I know you won't keep me here, the other foster parents haven't. You'll just let me stay for a while and you'll get tired of me too." Prior to pre-adolescence children tend to live a 'daily' existence, looking neither back or forward.

Through observation and interview, the researcher discovered that a significant destabilizing factor for youth, is the reassignment of children who have been in long- term foster care with one family. This is often done just as the youths reach the pre-adolescent stage of their development. Reassignment is often due to maladaptive behavior. The majority of maladaptive pre-adolescent behavior, is prompted either by latent inherited psychological problems (i.e., conduct disorder), or biological conditions (i.e., fetal abuse through drug or alcohol consumption (Kazdin, 1987, 69). Maladaptive behavior of this type begins to make its appearance at this crucial stage of development (ages 10-12). A large number of youths in care, come from backgrounds which make them vulnerable to these disorders. Kazdin describes conduct disorder as both inherited and stable (57, 67). It is a condition which does not diminish over time, but rather remains constant. As can be seen from the table in Appendix J, early onset occurs around 10-12 years of age, and thus coincides with the age given by foster parents "A" as the year in which they returned the foster child.

In many cases, because of the psychological state of these youths, they are unaware that their behavior is the major cause of their reassignment. This brings into question the feasibility of treatment under "reality therapy," as espoused by one of the agencies in this study.

Lastly, abuse, is a very significant factor contributing to social disaffection. The abuses experienced by youths in care, as in the case of Sherry G., not only promote disaffection, but increase the likelihood of antisocial personality disorder, as well. More stringent action should be taken against abusive parents and foster parents. In the case of Sherry G., a simple client plan, directing that the abusive foster parent should receive monthly counseling and refrain from pulling her hair and hitting her in the face, does little to persuade the caretaker of the seriousness of the damage being done to the ward. In some instances abuse is the consequence of a loss of patience, but it is more often the result of being unable to cope with the child, due to lack of respite.

What Role Does Contextual Environment (Home, Community and Peers) Play in Shaping the Realities of Minority Adolescents (i.e., Appropriate Behaviors as a Middle-Class Concept)?
In answering this question, the researcher focused her attention not on the youths' present environment, which is examined above. rather, she wanted to know how the child's former environment influenced his/her perception of what was presently taking place. Cartwright (1993), Rogers' (1959), and Sroufe & Waters (1977) agree that youths with behavioral problems, are more likely to misread environmental and interpersonal cues and become bullies, or exhibit behavior which is hostile. This is particularly so in instances where there is/has been a lack of maternal/paternal socialization.

As was discussed earlier, the concept of appropriate behavior is behavior, which allows the individual to function and survive in a particular environment. As an example, street behavior is inappropriate in school, just as school behavior is inappropriate in the street. Very few children who live in inner-city neighborhoods would survive on the street, if they adhered to what is seen as appropriate behavior in school, and the situation is reversed, when street behavior is performed in school.

As a response to this problem, and bearing in mind the studies of the above-cited researchers, the most appropriate action would be to make the youth aware, that each is appropriate in its place. For example, using inner-city survival tactics in rural areas, would be akin to wearing an evening gown with sneakers. The researcher has had a good deal of success in assisting students and clients to redirect their behavior so that it is employed in the appropriate environments. This was done without denigrating either behavior.

FOSTER CARE – RECOMMENDATIONS

Based on the above discussion, the researcher provides below several recommendations:

1. In group homes, every effort should be made to provide counselors and advisors who share the same ethnic background as the children in care.

2. If a minority youth is living in a community where there are
    no members of his/her ethnic group, efforts should be made to
    ensure that s/he participates in community programs in areas
    where s/he can associate with members of his/her own ethnic
    group. This should include participation in church-related
    activities, the PAL, crafts, drama, sports, or other activities
    where s/he is certain to find large numbers of people from
    his/her own ethnic background.
3. School, health and community programs should be balanced
    in their representation of minority members at decision-
    making levels and at the youth/mentor level.
4. If possible, every effort should be made to keep youths in their
    own communities and, more specifically, their own homes.
    The focus should be on family preservation, as opposed to
    exodusing youths outside of their communities to rural areas,
    where lifestyles, habits, and population differ. If this does
    become necessary, a concerted effort should be made to
    involve youths in community activities to ensure that
    resocialization occurs gradually. This can best be achieved by
    dispensing with the chicanery of trying to "sneak" a group
    home into an area. An attempt to integrate group homes into
    new areas, should include community cooperation.
    Community members should be advised of the proposed move
    to the area. Youths and community members should meet.
    Often, this will allay the fears the communities have about the
    people who are coming to the area. It is, after, all much easier
    to deny access to a faceless child than one with a face.
5. Community members should be invited to mentor, create
    programs for, and advise on ways that residents can improve
    the youths' chances of becoming useful members of the
    community in which they hope to form a part. Such efforts
    would negate the present system, which places youths in
    communities and then isolates them.
    By way of example, Pathmark supermarkets in Tobyhanna,
    Pennsylvania have joined in a community effort to help
    developmentally disabled adolescents both to obtain work and
    get to know the community in which they live. Once a week,

members of various group homes work in the Pathmark stores cleaning the shelves. The experience affords them the opportunity to work, observe, and speak to members of the community.

Another excellent example of community\youth cooperation program is that initiated by a group home director, who works with boys in need of out-of-home fostering. He designed a public relations program in which professional photographs were taken of youths and placed on the walls of Wendy's, calling attention to the need to provide the children with homes which were safe, warm, and caring.

6. To ensure foster parents' control of youths' behavior in their homes, the agency should clarify with foster adolescents, the status of the foster parents and the consequences of misbehavior. If not, parental authority is eroded and subservient to the will of the youth in care. A situation like this, can quite suddenly erupt in violence on the part of either party.

7. Agencies should make an attempt to increase the fee paid to foster parents. This would increase the number of available foster parents. The number of foster children allotted to each family should be reduced. The consequence would be that agencies could afford to be more selective. Second, it would alleviate the situation in which foster parents take more children than they can handle. Situations of this type are often attempts at small home businesses.

8. Since most programs require that one parent work, which in most instances, leaves the other at home, it is important that the resident parent participate in training which would provide an in-depth knowledge of how to work with children who have physical, emotional, or learning disabilities. To this end, the resident parent should not only be encouraged to enter courses on child development, but attendance at classes in psychology and first aid/practical nursing should be mandatory and cover a period of not less than two years. As was revealed by the foster parent interviews, the screening process for African-Americans was particularly stringent,

however, the researcher observed that in general, parent selection was somewhat questionable. This needs to be re-examined from the perspective of the minority child in care.

9. Parent/caseworker relationships could be improved by ensuring that the caseworker who visits a foster parent over age 45, is close to the foster parent's age. Age plays a significant role in creating animosity between caseworker and foster parent. Particularly if the caseworker has no experience with children at a personal level.

10. Caseworker/foster parent relations could also be improved if the caseworker earnestly tries to answer the questions the foster parent has, and balances his/her advice with candidness.

THE AGENCIES

The study discussed the fact that in some cases, smaller, private foster care systems may be inhibited in their effort to perform efficiently and effectively, by the number of subsidiary programs which they conduct in conjunction with the more significant task of providing foster care. Many of these programs either replicate those within their own organizations, or those existing under the organizational umbrellas of other agencies in the same area. Further study on the impact of diversification on effectiveness is required.

Diversification was originally designed with the intent of ensuring the perpetuation of the non-profit organization. However, as in the instance of the private foster care agency mentioned earlier, organizational energies are often expended in areas which show little benefit to the organization as a whole, or to the public. It might therefore be surmised that diversification may well be a means of boosting the amount of funding the organization can request when writing proposals.

When considering the role of the home, community, and peers in shaping the realities of minority adolescents, it would appear that little profit can be gained in terms of exodusing inner city youth. Despite the growth in out-of-home care agencies, the demand for care appears to be larger than the supply of both available shelter and adoptive/foster parents. The burgeoning numbers of displaced youth and the paucity of places available for them have led to reconsideration of orphanages as a means of accommodating the ever-increasing need for shelter and protection by young people. The National Broadcasting Corporation current events program, *60 Minutes* aired a segment on Sunday, July 30, 1995, on the question of the feasibility of reopening orphanages to accommodate large numbers of children and adolescents. The majority of support for this approach, has come from Speaker of the House, Newt Gingrich. He sees this alternative as the *ultimate solution* to youth vagrancy and displacement. The proposal is suspiciously eyed by religious and community leaders who fear the return of conditions as described by Charles Dickens in *Oliver Twist*. However, the crisis proportions of adolescents who are 'streeted" by the Department of Health and Human Services, and the number of child and infant abandonments, may soon demand that more assertive steps be taken to ensure that the existing conditions are brought under control. Cristina Szanton Blanc (1993), author of *Urban Children in Distress*, written on behalf of the United Nations Children's Fund, describes the child protective services situation as follows:

> Institutions dealing with children often have narrow preoccupations and compartmentalized concerns.
> The challenges faced today require comprehensive approaches and popular participation. Yet institutions which must meet those challenges tend to be independent and isolated from each other working within relatively narrow mandates and with closed decision-making processes. Institutions concerned with children's problems are cut off from those responsible for handling broader urban problems or for managing the overall economy. (3)

The points made in this brief analysis of the situation are well taken. Much of the exodusing of youth to rural areas has taken place without any advice from community development programs in the areas from which the foster children are taken. Yet those working in community programs in these stricken areas, are those most likely to be able to identify the problems and help in their solution. In isolating these organizations, and endeavoring to work the problem out alone, child protection agencies are making the same mistake that development agencies made in the 1960s in trying to resolve third world development, using a first world approach.

RECOMMENDATIONS

Paulo Friere (1972), a political scientist and educator, provides an apt example as to what should be taking place. Although the reference here is to education, the proposition can be applied well to the current the child protection services situation. He says, "Authentic education is not carried out by 'A' for 'B' or by 'A' about 'B', but rather by 'A' with 'B'. . ." (66)

Recently there has been an attempt among child protective services organizations to assist in the effort to support youths in their own homes. It is hoped that this approach will consider methods, which will:

(a) provide more respite and mental health care to parents with children who have emotional problems;

(b) provide respite to children who have parents with emotional problems ;

(c) begin/continue to expand upon programs which will provide closer liaison between community organizations providing after/before school programs; and

(d) involve community, parents, and educators in round table discussions on proposed methods for overcoming the necessity for long-term out-of-home care.

Additionally, there should be complete candidness about the psychological and physical states of children available for fostering. This can be facilitated, by requesting that foster parents provide monthly written reports. These could then be made available to the new foster parent on the reassignment of the youth. The reports should include detailed observations of behavior with respect to areas of cooperativeness, and habits which need improvement. Information as to various methods which have worked in directing the youth, as well as those which have failed, could also be noted. Some agencies do request these reports from foster parents, then keep them locked away from succeeding caretakers, making the information utterly useless. Psychological and physical profiles of the parents, as well as any information about existing relatives and their willingness to spend time with the youths, if appropriate, should also be made available to the foster parent, along with contact addresses.

Lastly the old fashioned notion of "distancing" must be eliminated from rules and regulations governing the behavior of protective services employees. Distancing serves only to alienate children who have already undergone severe conditions of alienation. If youths in protective services are unable to receive love and attention from their parents, from whom most have been removed, from teachers, who insist on maintaining a "professional distance;" and lastly, from foster parents and counselors, to whom are they going to go to fill the need for bonding? Unfortunately, the response is most generally peers, gangs, and groups. If significant others are distant, then it follows that youths who have been distanced will move in the direction of those from whom they can receive approval (see Figure at Appendix K). Social workers and significant others, are through the practice of distancing, creating a new generation of disaffected individuals by providing an environment which creates and nurtures antisocial behavior.

SPECIAL EDUCATION: SUMMARY, CONCLUSIONS, AND RECOMMENDATIONS

The researcher began the section on special education with her observations of student hunger. Student hunger is an indirect manifestation of the child protective services" failure to follow up on the health conditions of children in foster care and those living at or below poverty level. While it is conceivable that incidences of abuse will eventually come to the attention of the caseworkers, it is quite conceivable that few caseworkers attend to the question of proper nutrition. The reader will recall that family "B" stated that one of the children whom it fostered suffered from iron deficiency and had bad skin. These are strong indicators of poor nutrition. It is likely that a caseworker will ask a child whether s/he has ever been beaten by a foster parent, but is far less likely to ask whether s/he has ever been hungry. Since records of previous placements are expunged, and personal observations of behavior, likes and dislikes of foster children are not transmitted to the new foster parent by the previous foster parents, each reassignment requires that the new parents experiment with food to determine what foster youths will, or will not eat. The period of experimentation can prove detrimental to the health of foster youths who are at various stages of development.

Additionally, foster parents are in such fear of being viewed as child abusers, that they are often hesitant to exert the same disciplinary measures they would normally use with their own children. The consequence is that youths take advantage of this fear to exploit situations by challenging the power structure in the home. It is not unreasonable to assume a situation wherein the foster parent is told, "I'm not going to eat and you can't make me." This attitude has certainly been observed in the classroom with respect to other matters.

Although the situation is hypothetical, it draws on observations made by the researcher. The researcher contends that in many instances, attempts to prevent child abuse have resulted in powerless foster parents. Such regulations have done nothing to curb abuse. Abusive foster parents do what they like anyway, as in the case of Sherry G. Yet when abuse does occur, it would appear that the child protection services are almost totally powerless to do anything; action being contingent upon the availability to provide alternative shelter.

The researcher, in her efforts to investigate the numbers of students who come to school hungry and to find out how much hunger actually exists, was unable to get figures for children not placed on the school breakfast and lunch eligibility lists. Breakfast and lunch figures lend no insight into the number of students who are hungry because their parents are too proud to accept assistance. While foster children are normally placed on the lunch list, they are not always designated a place for the breakfast. It is assumed by the agency that these students will receive this meal at home, particularly since the families with whom they board are not categorized as falling below the poverty line—as is the case with the students on the breakfast program. In any case, student hunger is an area which requires much more research and the researcher highly recommends that this area be considered for further study.

The researcher would now like to sum up the findings on the attendance of foster care students in mainstream classes. Mainstream teachers at "A" level (i.e. library, arts and crafts, music, etc.) were all fully aware of the special problems of students in the special education classes. Most knew that students were either emotionally, mentally, or physically handicapped. They were not, however, aware of the students" domestic status. At "A" level this was irrelevant because the special arts teachers taught classes only when the teacher, or the teacher's aide accompanied students. In other words, in most instances, students at this level were taken as a class to participate in specific activities and were initially under the control of the special education teacher.

It is at "B" level that problems begin to surface. Of the responses provided to questionnaires circulated to mainstream teachers, the researcher found that the most common complaint these teachers had was that there were foster care students in their classes with domestic-related problems, of which they were unaware. They felt that there was a great need to be advised as to which students were in out-of-home care and as to the problems, if any connected with the foster assignment of the student.

One mainstream teacher advised that the cause of the problem-related behavior of one of her foster care students, was revealed to her by the natural parent (who was about to be incarcerated), as opposed to the foster parents. If the natural parent had not provided her with these insights, she would have had no idea of how to handle the student. Agency/teacher liaison does not occur at mainstream level, and foster parents are more likely to confer with the special education teacher. Foster parent/teacher liaison does not occur at mainstream level, therefore, unless the conditions in the classroom deteriorate to the point that parents are summoned to the school, no information is passed on. In some instances, repeated calls to attend parent/teacher, or administration/parent meetings regarding the foster child's disciplinary problems, have led to the return of the youth to protective services.

Another complaint voiced by both mainstream and special education teachers was that there had been incidences in which children were taken directly from the classroom by the child protective services and assigned to new foster homes without prior notice—as in the case of Marlene and her brother. This presented a difficult situation both for the students and the teacher, as there was no closure. Reassignment to new foster parents can also mean a change of school. Since it is very difficult to predict when this will occur, students are often removed from schools at crucial periods throughout the school year, which presents a situation of academic disruption.

In conclusion, the findings of the study revealed that there is no appreciable difference between the information provided to special education teachers and those who are mainstream. Some of the mainstream teachers stated that the only information they received which served to facilitate their classroom activities in respect of foster care students, was the IEP, which had been initiated by the special education teacher. However, special education teachers stated that IEPs drafted for these students had been designed without any input by the agency.

The normal practice was to test the students in all academic areas and then write an IEP for each student. After this was drafted, the teacher then met with the foster parent in order to discuss the IEP and if both parties agreed on the procedure, the IEP was signed. As can be observed from the foregoing, at no time during this process does the agency take an active part. Therefore, these plans are drafted and carried out without the input of the agency.

When asked what information would be of assistance in helping both mainstream and special education teachers to facilitate the instruction of foster care students, the responses were as follows:

TEACHERS' RECOMMENDATIONS ON WAYS TO ASSIST FOSTER CARE STUDENTS

1. All teachers wanted more information on the history and psychological state of the student. Many wanted more information on the natural parents. This included information as to whether the student was in contact with the natural parent. Additionally, information in respect of how long the student had been in foster care would also prove helpful in determining the causes for unexplained behavior.

2. Periodic progress report meetings regarding the student should be provided. If this was implemented, the student would benefit in that s/he would be aware that there was continual

communication between student, foster parent, caseworker and teacher.

3. Notification should be given to teachers both mainstream and special education of the status of foster care students before they arrive in class, together with information which would provide teachers with any insight pertaining to areas of sensitivity and/or special needs.

4. It was also felt that there should be more participation by the caseworker in the area of assessment and the provision of information which could be used to ensure that foster care students are placed in classes suited to their capacities.

5. Teachers also felt that the agency should be aware that teachers spend more time with foster care students than do agency personnel. In this regard teachers expected to meet and collaborate with the agencies more closely on the overall task of rehabilitation and education.

6. Teachers also felt that there should be periodic conferences and updates between the agency and the classroom teachers. Special classes and counseling sessions should be available for foster care students in the schools.

As can be concluded from the foregoing, the agency plays little or no role in ensuring that youth in care are provided with an education which will ensure that they will be capable of becoming individuals who can contribute to the role of society on reaching adulthood. The role of the agency and its shortcomings in this area is one which the researcher highly recommends for future research. The consequence of inadequate information and support in this area is certain to have a negative impact on the future of these youths and, consequently, weaken the social fabric of this country.

The study has afforded the researcher an opportunity to examine much of the mismanagement and disinterest which is occurring in the out-of-home care industry today. The seriousness with which the human services and child protection services undertake the handling of the task before them will determine the calibre and the ability to function of future citizens. At present, the future does not portend a positive outcome for youths in care. First of all, those working in this field must realize that the responsibility for this undertaking is one that must be held on many shoulders. At present, burnout, or the failure of superiors to acknowledge and commend the conscientious efforts of staff often extinguishes enthusiasm. Among the staff itself, attitudes range within the agencies, from "I'm glad it's not my child," to "what can I do, I'm only one person?" It should be remembered by those who say they are relieved because these not their children, that the youth in care today, will someday be interacting with their children in many different ways. The future of these children is in our hands. We can meet them at the level of their needs today, or we can meet them as criminal adversaries in the future.

Appendix A

Figure 1

Courtesy of Dodie Corpening and *Gifted, Created and Talented Magazine*

Appendix B

Pocono Record, Thursday, July 27, 1995
Page B-1

MOUNTAINHOME - The owners of two houses in Barrett Township being used as group foster homes say the municipality's zoning ordinances illegally ban the homes and the law should be changed.

Simultaneously, the same two houses are currently at the center of a zoning hearing board case, in which the township has claimed the homes were switched from single-family residential use without any application for proper permits and that the houses violate ordinances regulating home occupations in a residential zone.

A decision by the zoning hearing board is expected Aug. 7.

The two cases are not directly connected, according to Therese Hardiman, Barrett's special solicitor for zoning matters.

"They are independent proceedings," Hardiman said. "The decision in one may have very little to do with the decision in the other."

In papers dated July 12, H. Clark Connor, the attorney for the property owners and . . . , the non-profit agency operating the foster homes, proposed a curative amendment to the existing zoning code.

"Basically, what a curative amendment says is: 'I challenge your ordinance and this is the relief I want,'" Hardiman said.

The township supervisors can respond by agreeing with the application or holding hearings, then deciding whether or not their zoning code needs to be changed and how, Hardiman said.

The decision can be appealed in court.

The township and county planning commissions should first make a recommendation Connor said.

Barrett Township supervisors chairman James Manhart said the supervisors have not yet discussed their response to the curative amendment and don't expect to until after the zoning hearing board decision.

Hardiman said the township has been accused of "going after children," in their current zoning hearing board case.

While the zoning hearing board cannot put conditions on the homes, the township can. Hardiman said.

At last week's zoning hearing board session, Denise Leonard was asked by Hardiman if there would be any conditions that could be attached to the permit to make it acceptable to her.

Leonard said she's observed police calls, violence and children out of control at the house.

At an earlier session of the zoning hearing board other residents testified in favor of allowing the group homes.

Appendix C

Table 1.

*Percentage of children in out-of-home Care in the United
States According to Race*

Race	% of Children in Care	% of all Children in Care
African-American	34%	15%
Caucasian	48%	69%
Latino/a	9%	12%

Source: American Civil Liberties Foundation Fact Sheet, 1994.

Appendix D

Questionnaire for Minority Foster Mothers

1. Into what age bracket do you fit?
   30-39
   40-49
   50-59
2. What educational background or personal experience do you have which you feel qualifies you to be a foster mother?
3. Why did you decide to foster children?
4. Do you know of any other minority women fostering children in this area?
5. Can you approximate their ages?
6. Did you specifically request minority children?
7. If so, why?
8. Did the agency offer to give you non-minority children?
9. If so, what were the ages of the children offered?
10. Do you believe there is a racial bias in the way in which foster agencies offer children for fostering to minority foster parents?
11. Have you encountered this, if so explain.
12. What was/were the age/ages of the children given to you?
13. How many children have you fostered?
14. What were the sexes of your foster children?
15. How long was/were the child/children in your care?
16. What were the problems, if any, that you encountered in caring for the child/children in respect of behavior(s) and

(Use additional sheets to answer this question if necessary)

17. Do you feel the agency told you about all the facts regarding the child's behavior and background?

18. If not, how did this affect the relationship you had with the child?

19. Did this result in the return of the child/children? If so, explain (Use additional pages attached for response if necessary)

20. Describe the type of relationship you have/had with the agency, caseworker and administrative staff.

21. Was this a factor in returning the child/children?

22. Do you feel that the agency acted responsibly in assisting you in matters concerned with the care of the child/children (i.e. providing you with adequate respite, money to cover unanticipated expenses and in resolving problem behavior)? (Additional pages are provided for this question)

23. Does the agency respond quickly to the immediate needs of the child?

24. Does the agency provide opportunities for you and the biological parents to discuss the child's problem and/or behavior?

25. Was the child, if from a minority background, aware of his/her ethnicity?

26. Had the children been fostered by a non-minority family prior to coming to stay with you, if so, how long?

27. What, if any in terms of physical appearance or behavior performed by the child indicated t hat he/she. had been neglected, or that s/he was unaware of his/her ethnicity?

28. Did the child perform any behavior which indicated that there had been a lack of nurturing such as stiffening on being embraced, or pushing away from any attempt which indicated a show of affection?

29. Did the child's developmental age correspond positively with his/her chronological age? In other words, did the child appear to know what s/he should know at this stage of his/her development?

30. What was the relationship between the child's caseworker, yourself and the child?
31. Have you any comments or criticisms you would like to make about the agency, or its staff?
33. Is your agency a local Pennsylvania agency or a tri-state agency, if a tri-state agency, which state.
34. At the schools attended by your foster children, are there any minority people holding professional positions, such as certified teachers, social workers, nurses mental health workers, or speech pathologists?
35. Are you a native of the rural Pennsylvania area or have you relocated to this area?
36. If you have relocated to this area, what are your perceptions of child care and adolescent education as it affects minority children.

Appendix E

Table 2.

Symptoms Included in the Diagnosis of Conduct Disorder

A period of six months or more during which some number of the following behaviors are evident. Specifically the child or adolescent

1. is frequently truant
2. often "borrows" things from others without their permission
3. cheats in games with others or in school work
4. runs away (at least twice) from home (but not in reaction to physical or sexual abuse)
5. frequently initiates fights
6. has used a weapon in more than one fight
7. has forced someone into sexual activity
8. has been physically cruel to animals
9. has been physically cruel to other people
10. has deliberately destroyed property of others
11. has deliberately engaged in firesetting

Table 2. Continued

12. has had voluntary sexual intercourse unusually early for his or her subculture
13. regularly uses tobacco, liquor, or other nonprescribed drugs and began their use usually early
14. often lies in situations other than to avoid physical or sexual abuse
15. has broken into someone else's house, building or car
16. has stolen outside of the home without confronting a victim on more than one occasion
17. has stolen outside of the home with confrontation of a victim

SOURCE: Alan E Kazdin (1987) *Conduct Disorder in Childhood and Adolescence,* Newbury Park CA: Sage Publications.

Appendix F

Table 3.

Key Worker- Client Relationship Competencies as Identified by Child Welfare Clients

Workers must show clients basic human respect.

Workers must not be pushy or rude.

Workers must ask permission of clients to look in rooms or examine contents of cupboard.

Workers must be willing to spend time with clients.

Workers must be consistently honest with clients.

Workers must be aware of the dehumanizing context of child welfare work

Workers must be able to effectively communicate with clients.

Workers must speak at the client's level.

Workers must use direct language.

Workers must be able to really listen to what the client says.

Workers should be able to use small talk as an aid to establishing effective communication.

Workers must be able to develop a comfortable relationship with clients.

Workers should have an ability to develop relationships that are warm, not simply non hostile.

Workers must be able to cast themselves as a friend and an asset to the client.

Workers must use an emphatic presentation.

Workers must not prejudge families on the basis of reports from other workers or the nature of the initial report.

Workers must have the ability to remain calm and to defuse client anger, especially in initial meetings.

SOURCE: Drake, Brett (1994). *Relationship Competencies in Child Welfare Services. Social Work, 39, 5.*

Appendix G

1. Do you have foster children in your class, if so, how many and are they minority children?
2. Have you found them to be more difficult than children who come from homes where they live with their natural parents?
3. If so, were you advised by the agency of the behavioral problems the student might present?
4. Do you attend IEP meetings on children in foster care, or does the agency and the foster parent participate in meetings without you?
5. What information do you feel you should know that would help you to work with foster children who are students?
6. Would you like to/or do you meet often with caseworkers in regard to the foster children in your class?
7. Do you have any suggestions as to what you feel the agency might do in respect of your task of educating these students which might make your job easier and place the student in a more comfortable position?

Appendix H

Figure 2

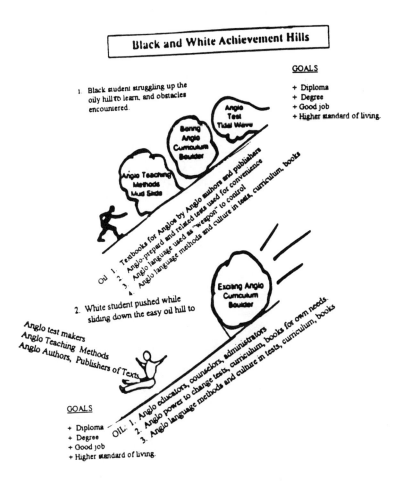

SOURCE: Alton D. Rison (1992). *How to teach African-American children.* Sarasota Florida: Sunbelt Theatre Productions Inc.

Appendix I

PREGNANCY PROFILE

Figure 3

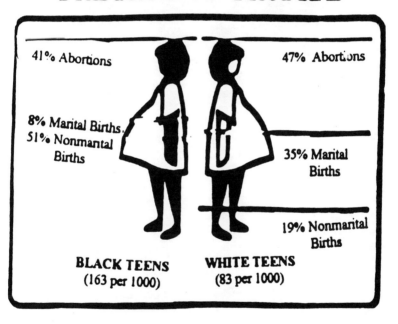

PREGNANCY PROFILE

41% Abortions

47% Abortions

8% Marital Births.
51% Nonmarital
Births

35% Marital
Births

19% Nonmarital
Births

BLACK TEENS
(163 per 1000)

WHITE TEENS
(83 per 1000)

Magid, K. , & Mckelvey, C.A. (1989) *High risk: Children without conscience.* New York: Bantam Books

Appendix J

Table 4

Characteristics that Predict Continued Antisocial Behavior in Adulthood

Characteristic	Specific Pattern
1. Age of Onset	Earlier onset (e.g. before 10 or 12) of their antisocial behavior. Early onset also is related to rate and seriousness of later antisocial behavior
2. Breadth of Deviance	A greater number of different types of antisocial behaviors; a greater variety of situations in which antisocial behavior is manifest (e.g., at home, school); a greater range of persons or organizations against whom such behaviors are expressed.
3. Frequency of Antisocial Behavior	A greater number of different antisocial episodes independently of whether they includes a number of different behaviors
4. Seriousness of the Behavior	Relatively serious antisocial behavior in childhood, especially if the behavior could be grounds for

Table 4 (Continued)

	adjudication
5. Type of Symptoms	The following specific antisocial behaviors: lying, impulsiveness, truancy, running away, theft, and staying out late. Also if they show non-antisocial symptoms of slovenliness and enuresis (after age 6)
6. Parent Characteristics	Parent psychopathology, particularly if antisocial behavior; father has record of arrest, unemployment, alcoholism; poor parental supervision of child; overly strict, lax or inconsistent discipline
7. Family	Greater if from homes with marital discord and larger family size

Kazdin, Alan E (1987). *Conduct Disorders in Childhood and Adolescence*. (p. 66). Newbury Park, CA: Sage Publications.

Appendix K

Figure 4.

A Progressive Model of Antisocial Behavior

Early childhood	Middle childhood	Late childhood	Pre adolescence	Adolescence

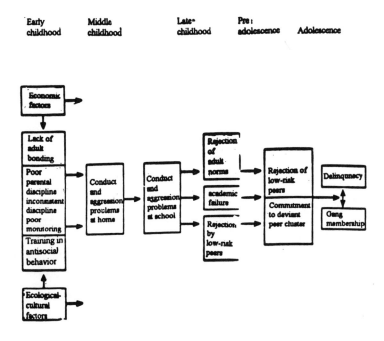

SOURCE: Drawn in Part from Patterson, De Beryshe, & Ramsey, 1989

VI

Definition of Terms

Adolescent. Clients aged 13-21

Age out. Attain legal adulthood (18 years) and thus no longer remain the responsibility of the child protective services.

Antisocial Personality Disorder (APD). A serious mental disorder experienced by individuals over the age of 18, which is traceable to the earlier condition, conduct disorder. The individual lacks affection, respect for others and society in general; is egocentric, manipulative can be homicidal and cannot be trusted (see American Psychiatric Association's Diagnostic and Statistical Manual of Mental Disorders IV under the same heading [1994].)

Children. Individuals under age 12.

Conduct Disorder (CD). Predecessor to the more serious mental condition of antisocial personality disorder. Is most often   seen   in younger people who have a potential for it to stabilize into APD in adulthood (see American Psychiatric Association's Diagnostic and Statistical Manual IV under the same heading [1994].)

Department of Children & Youth (C & Y). Local child welfare department reporting to the DHS and DPW.

Drug Rebound. In this instance, the condition of relapse relating to the wearing off of the effects of Ritalin in hyperactive children.

Exodus Programs. Those foster or group home care programs which are designed to remove the child from the inner city to rural areas.

Expectation Formation. A response by the subject which s/he believes the significant other anticipates.

Foster Care. Group home for temporary care in a setting outside the home.

Foster Parents. Those individuals providing child care for payment on a 24-hour basis with the same client, in their homes.

Group Homes. Residences in which 3 or more same-sex adolescents live.

Minority. Clients who are not Caucasian and more specifically either African-American or Hispanic.

Multiple Personalities (MP). A mental disorder in which the individual actually lives out and experiences his/herself as other personalities, taking on different identities, roles, and behaviors for varying periods of time. Often upon recovering self at the close of such episodes, is unable to remember what has occurred over extended periods of time.

Out-of-Home Care. Any residential care given to youth which is not undertaken in the natural home environment.

Streeted/Streeting. In the first instance it means to return adolescents to the streets and advise them to use their own devices to keep alive. In the second instance it means the process of multiple placements for young children due to lack of the availability of long-term shelter.

Youth. A term to represent young people of both categories (child/adolescent).

Bibliography

* References marked with an asterisk indicate studies included in the meta-analysis.

*Abraham, H.J. *Freedom and the court: civil rights and liberties in the United States (5th ed.)*. New York: Oxford University Press, 1988.

*Adelman, I. A poverty-focused approach to development policy. In J. P. Lewis and V. Kallab (Eds.) *Development strategies reconsidered New Brunswick, NJ: Transaction Book, 1986*.

Alexis, M. and G.R. Hendersen. The economic base of African-American communities: A study of consumption patterns. In B.J. Tidwell (ed.) *The state of African-American America 1994* New York: National Urban League.

Allport, G.W. *Becoming: basic considerations for a psychology of personality.* New Haven, CT.: Yale Press, 1955.

American Civil Liberties Foundation. *Children's rights project (Case summaries)*. New York: Author, December, 1994.

*American Civil Liberties Union Foundation. Children's rights fact sheet. New York: Author, 1993

*American Civil Liberties Union. *A force for change: children's rights project of the ACLU.* New York: Author, 1993.

American Psychiatric Association. *Diagnostic and statistical manual of mental disorders* (4th ed.). Washington, D.C.: Author, 1994.

Anderson, E. *Street wise: Race, class and change in an urban community.* Chicago, IL: University of Chicago Press, 1990.

Andreasen, N. *The broken brain: The biological revolution in psychiatry.* New York: Harper & Row, 1984.

Appiah, K.A. Straightening out the bell curve. In R. Jacoby and N. Glauberman (eds.) *The bell curve debate.* New York: Times Books, 1995.

Asbury, C.A., Walker, S, Belgrave, F.Z., Maholmes, V. & Green, L. Psychological, cultural, and accessibility factors associated with participation of African-Americans in rehabilitation. ` *Rehabilitation Psychology,* 39 (2), 1994.

*Auletta, K *The underclass.* New York: Random House, 1983.

*Baby Neal, et al. Vs. Robert P. Casey, Defendants.,No. 90-2343 (Court of Common Pleas, PA. 1992.)

Barnett, D.W. and C.B. Zucker. *The personal and social assessment of children: An analysis of current status and professional practice issues.* Needham, MA: Allyn & Bacon, 1990.

Bar Tal, D. Interactions of teachers and pupils. In I.H. Frieze, D. Bar Tal and J.S. Carroll (eds.) *New approaches to social problems.* San Francisco: Jossey-Bass, 1979.

*Barth, R On their own: The experiences of youth after foster care. *Child and Adolescent Social Work Journal 7,* 1993.

*Becnel, B. C. Poverty as policy. *Essence Magazine,* December, 1993.

Bell, C.C. and E.J. Jenkins. Community violence and children on Chicago's southside *Psychiatry, 56,* February, 1993.

Berry, K.D. Adoption race and red tape. *Emerge Magazine.* April, 1995.

Bettis, P.J., H.C. Cooks and D.A. Bergin. It's not steps anymore, but more like shuffling': Student perceptions of the civil rights movement and ethnic identity. *Journal of Negro Education, 63.* 1994.

Bereiter, C. Jensen and educational differences. In *The Bell Curve Debate.* Russell Jacoby and Naomi Glauberman (eds.) New York: Times Books, 1995.

Blauner, B. *Black lives, white lives: Three decades of race relations in America.* Berkeley CA: University of California Press, 1990.

*Blechman, E.A. Mentors for high-risk minority youth: From effective communication to bicultural competence. *Journal of Clinical Child Psychology, 21* (2), 1992.

*Bowditch, C. Getting rid of troublemakers: High school disciplinary procedures and the production of dropouts. *Social Problems, 40* (4),. November, 1993.

*Boyd-Franklin, N. *African-American families in therapy: A multi-systems approach.* New York: Guilford, 1989.

Bremner, R.H. Child welfare in fiction and fact. *Child Welfare* 74 (1), January/February, 1995.

Buchman, M. Role over person: Legitimacy and authenticity in teaching. In M. Ben-Peretz, R. Bromme and R. Halkes. *Advances of research in teacher thinking.* Lisse, Switzerland: Swets & Zeitlinger, 1986.

Carrier, J.G. *Learning disability: Social class and the construction of inequality in American education.* Westport, CT.: Greenwood Press, 1986.

*Carson, C., D.J. Garrow, D.J., V. Harding and D.C. Hine. *Eyes on the prize* . New York: Penguin Books, 1987.

*Cartwright, M. and M. D'Orso. *For the children.* New York: Doubleday, 1993.

*Chalmer, E.T. and S.T. Jenal. Interracial and intraracial quasi-counseling interactions when counselors avoid discussing race. *Journal of Counseling Psychology, 41* (4), 1994.

*Children's Defense Fund. *Children's Defense Fund   Yearbook 1997.* Washington, D.C.

*Chiles, N. Making schools work.(An interview with Dr. James P. Comer, professor of child psychiatry and associate dean at the Yale Medical School.) *Essence Magazine,* December, 1993.

Clark, C.X. The Shockley-Jensen thesis: A contextual appraisal. *The African-American Scholar,* July/August, 1973.

Coleman, H. Cleman, L.K. Wampold, B.E. and S.L. Casali, S.L Ethnic minorities' ratings of ethnically similar and European American counselors: A meta-analysis. *Journal of Counseling Psychology,* 1995.

*Comer, J.P. Educating poor minority children *Scientific American* 259 (5), November, 1988.

Comer, J.P. *A brief history and summary of the school development program 1993-94* . New Haven, CT: Yale Child Study Center, 1994.

Conger, J.J. and A.C. Petersen. *Adolescent and youth: Psychological development in a changing world* (3rd ed.) New York: Harper and Row, 1984.

*Cose, E. *The rage of a privileged class.* New York: Harper Perennial, 1993.

Cottman, B.B. Poverty as a policy. *Essence Magazine,* 1993, December.

*Courtney, M.E. and R.C. Collins. New challenges and opportunities in child welfare outcomes and information Technologies. *Child Welfare* 73 (5), Sept/Oct., 1994.

Crittenden, P.M. and M.D.S. Ainsworth. *Child maltreatment and attachment theory.* Chiccheti S. & V.Carlson (eds.) Child maltreatment: Theory and research on the causes and consequences of child abuse and neglect. Cambridge MA: Cambridge University Press, 1989.

Dardo, D. and K. McCurdy. Preventing child abuse and neglect: Programmatic interventions *Child Welfare Vol. 73* (5), .Sept/Oct., 1994.

Davis, L. E., M.J. Galinsky and J.H. Schopler. RAP: A framework for leadership of multiracial groups. *Social Work 40* (2), March, 1995.

Dodge, K.A. Attributional bias in aggressive children. In P. C. Kendall (ed.), *Advances in Cognitive-Behavioral Research and Therapy Vol. 4*. Orlando, FL: Academic Press, 1985.

Doren, D. *Understanding and treating the psychopath*. New York. Wiley & Sons, 1987.

*Drake, B. Relationship competencies in child welfare services. *Social Work 39* (5), September, 1994.

*Dryfoos, Joy G. Adolescents at risk: A summation of work in the field— programs and policies. *Journal of Adolescent Health*, 1991, September.

English, Diana J. and Peter J. Pecora. Risk assessment as a practice method in child protective services. *Child Welfare 73 5*, Sept/Oct, 1994.

*Fanshel, D., S. Finch and J. Grundy. *Foster children in a life course perspective*. New York: Columbia University Press. 1990.

*Feagin, J.R. and N. Imani. Racial barriers to African-American entrepreneurship: An explanatory study *Journal of African-American Psychology*, November, 1994.

Feldman, R.S. and R. Saletsky. Non-verbal communication in racial teacher-student interaction. In. R.S. Feldman (ed.), *The social psychology of education: Current research and theory*. Cambridge: Cambridge University Press, 1986.

*Festinger, T. No one ever asked us. . .*A postscript to foster care*. New York: Columbia University Press, 1983.

Ford, Robert C. *Counseling strategies for ethnic minority students*. Tacoma, WA: University Puget Sound Bookstore, 1986.

Friendship House Children's Center. *Specialized Treatment Family Foster Care Program*. [Information Packet]. Ackourey, P: Author, 1993.

*Friere, P. *Pedagogy of the oppressed*. New York: Penguin Books, 1972.

Goerge R., F. Wulczyn and Fanshel, D. A foster care research agenda for the '90s. Child Welfare 7 (5), 1994.

Gibbs, N. R. Murder in miniature. *Time Magazine*, September, 1994.

Gibbs, N.R. The vicious cycle. *Time Magazine*, June 20, 1994.

Gibbs, J.T. and L.N. Huang, (eds.) *Children of color: Psychological interventions with minority youth*. San Francisco, CA: Jossey-Bass, 1989.

*Giusti, A.L. Breakpoint and beyond: Youth violence. Paper presented at the Walden University Regional Intensive Seminars, Washington, D.C., December, 1994.

*Glasgow, D.G. *The African-American underclass: Poverty, unemployment and entrapment of ghetto youth*. New York: Jossey-Bass Inc., 1980.

Goldstein, J., A. Freud and A.J. Solnit. *Before the interests of the child.* New York: The Free Press, 1979.

Goldstein, J.A. Freud and A.J. Solnit. *Beyond the interests of the child.* New York: Free Press, 1973.

Graham, S. An attributional perspective on achievement motivation and African-American children. In. R.S. Feldman (ed.). *The social psychology of education: Current research and theory.* Cambridge: Cambridge University Press, 1986.

Grier, W.H. and P.M. Cobbs. *African-American rage.* New York: Basic Books, 1968.

Hagan, J. Labeling and Deviance: A case study in sociology of the interesting. Social Problems 20, 1973.

Hale-Benson, J.E. *African-American Children: Their roots, culture and learning styles (Rev. ed.).* Baltimore, MD: John Hopkins Press, 1982.

Hallowell, E.M. and J.J. Ratey. *Driven to distraction: Recognizing and coping with attention deficit disorder from childhood through adulthood.* New York: Pantheon Books, 1994.

Hargreaves, D.H. *Deviance in classrooms.* London: Routledge & Kegan Paul, 1975.

Haring, N.G. and E.L. Phillips. *Educating emotionally disturbed children.* New York: McGraw-Hill, 1962.

Hartmann, T. *Attention deficit disorder: A different perception.* Penn Valley, CA: Underwood-Miller, 1993.

*Haynes, N.M. *Critical issues in educating African-American children.* Langley Park, MD: IAAS Publishers, 1993.

*Healy, J.M. *Endangered minds: Why our children don't think.* New York: Touchstone Books, 1990.

Heath, S.B. and M.W. McLaughlin. *Identity and inner city youth.* New York: Teachers' College Press, 1993.

Henderson, L.J. African-Americans in the urban milieu: Conditions, trends and development needs B.J. Tidwell (ed.) *State of African-American America* New York: National Urban League, 1994.

*Henggeler, S.W. *Delinquency in adolescence.* Newbury Park, CA: Sage Publication. Hester, G. and B. Nygren. (1981) Child of rage. Nashville, TN: Thomas Nelson, 1989.

*Hill, R. *Research on the African-American family.* Westport, CT: Auburn House, 1993.

Holmes, S.A.I. Bitter racial dispute rages over adoption: White couple seeks custody of 2 African-Americans. *New York Times,* A16. April 13, 1995.

Hutchinson, E.O. *The assassination of the African-American male image.* Los Angeles, CA: Middle Passage Press, 1994.

*Johnson, K. Alive and well. *Essence Magazine*, December, 1993.

Jones, B.E. Major affective disorders in African-Americans: A preliminary report. *Integral Psychiatry*, 1988.

Jones, D. J. and G. Harrison. Comparative Views of African-American status and progress *The State of African-American America.* New York: National Urban League, 1994.

Kagan, J. Etiologies of adolescents at risk. *Journal of Adolescent Health 12,* 1991.

*Katz, M. B. *The undeserving poor.* New York: Pantheon Books, 1989.

*Kazdin, A.E. *Conduct disorders in childhood and adolescence.* Newbury Park CA: Sage Publications, 1987.

*Kazdin, A.E. Adolescent mental health: prevention and treatment programs. *American Psychologist,* 1993, February.

Kelling, G.W. *Language: Mirror, tool, and weapon.* Chicago: Nelson Hall.

Kendall, P.C. and L. Braswell. (1985*). *Cognitive-behavioral therapy for impulsive children.* New York: Guilford, 1975.

*Kotlowitz, A. *There are no children here.* New York: Doubleday, 1991.

*Kozol, J. *Savage inequalities: Children in America's schools.* New York, Harper Collins Books, 1991.

*Kozol, J. *Death at an early age.* New York: Penguin Books, 1967.

Kugelmass, J. *Behavior, bias, and handicaps: labeling the emotionally disturbed child.* New Brunswick, N.J.: Transaction Books, 1987.

*Leung, P., K.F. Cheung and K.M. Stevenson. A strengths approach to ethnically sensitive practice for child protective service workers. *Child Welfare* 73 (6), Nov/Dec., 1994.

*Magid, K. and C.A. McKelvey. *High risk: Children without conscience.* New York: Bantam Books, 1989.

*Marks, C. *Farewell—we're good and gone: The great African-American migration.* Bloomington IN: Indiana University Press, 1989.

*Martin, T.W. White therapists' differing perceptions of African-American and white adolescents. *Adolescence* 28, Summer, 1993.

*Mason, J. and C. Williams. The adoption of minority children: Issues in developing law and policy. In *Adoption of children with special needs: Issues in law and policy.* Washington, DC: American Bar Association, 1985.

Massat, R.C. Is older better? Adolescent parenthood and maltreatment *Child Welfare 74.* (2), Mar/Apr., 1995.

*Massey, D.S. and N.A. Denton. *American apartheid: segregation and the making of the underclass.* Cambridge, MA: Harvard University Press, 1993.

*Maughan, B. Childhood precursors of aggressive offending in personality-disordered adults. In Sheilagh Hadgins (ed.) *Mental Disorder and Crime* Newbury Park: CA: Sage Publications, 1993.

McDonald, M.J. The citizen's committee for children of New York and the evolution of child advocacy (1945-1972). *Child Welfare.* 74 (1), January/February, 1995.

*McGuiness, D. *When children don't learn.* New York: Basic Books, 1985.

*McWhirter, J.J. *At-risk youth: A comprehensive response.* Pacific Grove, CA: Brooks/Cole Publishing, 1993.

*Meadwcroft, P., B. Thomlison, and P. Chamberlain. Treatment foster care services: A research agenda for welfare *Child Welfare 73* (5), Sept./Oct., 1994.

*Mech, E. Foster youths in transition: research perspectives on preparation for independent living. *Child Welfare 73* (5), Sept./Oct., 1994.

*Mehan, H. The role of language and the language of role in institutional decision making *Language in Society,* 12, 1983.

Meier, E. Current circumstances of former foster children. *Child Welfare 44,* 1965.

*Mellor, J.W. Agriculture on the road to industrialization Lewis, J. P. and Kallab, V. (eds.) (pp. 67-89.) In *Development strategies reconsidered.* (67-87) New Brunswick, N.J.: Transaction Books, 1986.

Minerbrook, S. Home ownership anchors the middle class *Emerge Magazine,* 42, October, 1993.

National Urban League 80th Anniversary 1910-1990 New York: National Urban League, 1995.

*North American Council on Adoptable Children. *Barriers to same race placement.* St. Paul MN.: Author, 1991

O'Hare, W. P. African-Americans in the 1990s. *Population Bulletin 46* (1), 2-37, July, 1991.

*Osmond, M. The treatment foster care program for the Children's Aid Societies of Durham, Kawartha-Haliburton and Northumberland. Coburg, ON: Ontario Association of Children's Aid Societies and the Ministry of Community and Social Services. 1992.

Paterson, G.R. An early starter model for predicting delinquency. In D. Pepler and K.H. Rubin (eds.) *The development and treatment of childhood aggression.* Hilldale N.J. :Lawrence Erlbaum, 1991.

Paterson, G.R.& Reid, J.B. Social interactional processes within the family: The study of moment-by-moment family transaction in which human development is imbedded. *Journal of Consulting and Clinical Psychology, 5,* 1984.

Payette, K. A. and H.F. Clarizo. Discrepant team decisions: The effects of race, gender, achievement, and IQ on LD eligibility *Psychology in the Schools, 31,* January, 1994.

*Payne, R. S. The relationship between teachers' beliefs and sense of efficacy and their significance to urban LSES minority students. *Journal of Negro Education, 63* (2), 1994.

*Pecora, P. J., J.K. Whittaker & A.N. Maluccio. *The child welfare challenge: Policy, practice and research.* New York: Aldine de Gruyter, 1992.

*Penzerro, R. M. and L. Lein. Burning their bridges: Disordered attachment and foster care discharge. *Child Welfare, 74* (2), Mar./Apr., 1995.

Peoples, B. Civil rights report card. *Emerge Magazine,* March, 1995.

*Petrich, J. Rate of psychiatric morbidity in a metropolitan county jail population. *American Journal of Psychiatry,* 133, 1976.

Powledge, F. *The new adoption maze.* St. Louis, MO: C.V. Mosby, 1985.

Price, H. B. Keynote address. Paper presented at the National Urban League Convention, Indianapolis, Indiana, July 24, 1994.

Price, H.B. Keynote address. presented at the National Urban League Fortune 500 Forum, New York, November 4, 1994.

*Proctor, E. K. and L.E. Davis The challenge of racial difference: Skills for clinical practice. *Social Work 39* (3), May, 1994.

Ramirez, M., III. *Psychotherapy and counseling with minorities.* Needham Heights, MA: Allyn and Bacon, 1994.

Rasberry, W. The limits of IQ In R. Jacoby and N. Glauberman (eds.) *The Bell Curve Debate.* New York: Times Books, 1995.

*Redkey, E.S. *African-American exodus: African-American nationalist and back-to-Africa movements 1890-1910.* New Haven, CT: Yale University Press, 1969.

Renkin, B. Early childhood antecedents of aggression and passive-withdrawal in early elementary school. *Journal of Personality,* 57, 1989.

Rickel, A.U. and L. Allen, *Preventing maladjustment from infancy through adolescence.* Newbury Park, CA: Sage Publication, 1987.

Ridley, C.R., D.W. Mendoza, B.E. Kanitz, L. Angermeier, and R. Zenk. (1994). Cultural sensitivity in multicultural counseling: A perceptual schema model. Journal of *Counseling Psychology, 41* (2), 1989.

*Rison, A.D. *How to teach African-American children* (rev. ed.) Sarasota, FL: Sunbelt Theatre Productions Inc., 1992.

*Ritter, B. *Sometimes God has a kid's face.* New York: Covenant House, 1988.

*Robinson, L. Curbing a sick practice: An interview with Hazel R. O'Leary, Secretary, US Dept of Energy on January 22, 1993. *Emerge Magazine,* October, 1994.

*Rodriguez, P. and A. Meyer. Minority adoptions and agency practices. *Social Work, 35,* 1990.

*Rogers, C.R A theory of therapy, personality, and interpersonal relationships as developed in the client-centered framework. In S. Koch (ed.) *Psychology: A Study of a Science. 3.* New York: McGraw-Hill, 1959.

Rogers, C.R. *A way of being* (rev. ed.) Boston, MA: Houghton Mifflin, 1980.

*Ropers, R.H. *Persistent poverty: The American dream turned nightmare.* New York: Plenum Press, 1991.

Rowe, D.C., A.T. Vazsonyi, and D.J. Flannery. No more than skin deep: Ethnic and racial similarity in developmental process. *Psychological Review,* 101 (3), 1994.

*Rubin, R.H., A. Billingsley & C.H. Caldwell. The role of the African-American church in working with African-American adolescents. *Adolescence, 29* (114), Summer, 1994.

Rutter, M. *Maternal deprivation reassessed.* New York: Penguin Books, 1981.

Scalera, N.R. The critical need for specialized health and safety measures for child welfare workers. *Child Welfare,* 74 (2), Mar./Apr., 1995.

Schinke, S.P., G.J. Botvin, and M.A. Orlandi. *Substance abuse in children and adolescents: Evaluation and Intervention.* Newbury Park, CA: Sage Publications, 1991.

*Schulz, D.A. *Coming up African-American: Patterns of ghetto socialization.* Englewood Cliffs, N.J.: Prentice Hall, 1969.

*Serwatka, T.S. Disproportionate representation of African-Americans in emotionally handicapped classes. *Journal of African-American Studies, 25* (4), March, 1995.

*Sheehan, S. *Life for me ain't been no crystal stair.* New York: Pantheon Books, 1993.

*Shihadeh, E.S. and D.J. Steffensmeier. Economic inequality, family disruption and urban African-American violence: Cities as units of stratification and social control. *Social Forces, 73* (2), December, 1994.

*Simms, M.D. and N. Halfon. The health care needs of children in foster care: A research agenda. *Child Welfare,. 73* (5), Sept./Oct., 1994.

Sowell, T. *Civil rights: Rhetoric or reality.* New York: Quill, William, & Morrow, 1984.

*Sroufe, L.A. and B. Egeland. Illustrations of person-environment interaction from a longitudinal study. In T. Wachs and R. Plomin (eds.) *Conceptualization and measurement of organism-environmental interaction* Washington D.C.: American Psychological Association, 1991.

*Stehno, S. Kaleidoscope's youth development program: A last Chance for youth "aging out" of foster care. *Children Today, 16,* 1987.

Sue, S. Community mental health services for ethnic minority groups: A test of cultural responsiveness hypothesis. *Journal of Consulting and Clinical Psychology, 59,* 1991.

Sue, S. and N. Zane. The role of culture and cultural techniques in psychotherapy: A critique and reformulation. *American Psychologist,42* (1) January, 1987.

Terrell, F., S.L. Terrell, S.L. and F. Miler, F. Level of cultural mistrust as a function of educational and occupational expectations among African-American students *Adolescence, 28* (111), Fall,1993.

Thomas, M.E. Discrimination over the life course: A synthetic cohort analysis of earnings differences between African-American and white males 1940-1990. *Social Problems, 41* (4), November, 1994.

*Thomlison, B. and Y. Unrau. Exploring the service experiences from traditional and therapeutic foster parents" perspectives. Presented at the 7th Annual Foster Family-based Treatment Association Conference, Chicago, IL., August 9-13, 1993.

*Thompson, C.E. and S.T. Jenal. Interracial and intraracial quasi -counseling interactions when counselors avoid discussing race. *Journal of Counseling Psychology, 41.* (4), 1994.

Trescott, J. A sense of self. *Emerge Magazine*, March,1995.

Valocchi, S. The racial basis of capitalism and the state, and the impact of the new deal on African-Americans. *Social Problems, 41* (3), August, 1994.

Vidal, A. C. *Rebuilding communities: A national study of urban community development corporations.* New York: New School for Social Research, 1992.

Wallace-Benjamin, J. Organizing African-American self development: The role of community-based organizations. In B.J. Tidwell (ed.*) The State of African-American America 1994* New York: National Urban League, 1994.

Walters, R. Serving the People: African-American leadership and the challenge of empowerment. In B.J. Tidwell (ed.). *The State of African-American America 1994* New York: National Urban League, 1994.

Washington, H. Straightening out the bell curve. *Emerge Magazine,.* 28-31

*Washington, H. Human guinea pig. *Emerge Magazine*, Deember/January,1995.

Watson, M. F. and H. Protinsky. Identity status of African-American adolescents: An empirical investigation. *Adolescence, 26* (104), Winter, 1991.

West, C. *Race Matters* Boston, MA: Beacon Press, 1993.

White, J.L. *The psychology of African-Americans: An African-American perspective.* Englewood Cliffs, N.J.: Prentice Hall, 1984.

*Whittaker, J.K. and S.I. Pfeiffer. Research priorities for residential group care. *Child Welfare, 73* (5), Sept./Oct.,1994.

Williams, L.F. Targeting welfare. *Emerge Magazine,* April, 1995.

William, T. *The crack-cocaine context.* New York: Addison-Wesley Publishing Co., Inc., 1992.

*Willwerth, J. Madness in fine print *Time Magazine,* November 7, 1994.

Wilson, J.Q. & R.J.C. Herrenstein. (1985).*Crime and human nature.* New York: Simon & Schuster. M.D. Wilson, M. Kastrinakis, L.J. D'Angelo & P. Getson, Attitudes, knowledge and behavior regarding condom use in urban African-American adolescent males. *Adolescence, 29* (113). 1994, Spring.

*Wilson, W.J. *The truly disadvantaged.* Chicago: University of Chicago Press, 1990.

*Winborne, D. G. & P. Dardaine- Ragguet. Affective education for "at-risk" students: The view of urban principals. *The Urban Review, 25* (2), 1993.

Wolins, M. *Group care: Explorations in the powerful environment.* New York: Aldine Publishing Co., 1974.

Wysong, E. Truth and DARE: Tracking drug education to graduation and as symbolic politics. *Social Problems, 41* (3), August, 1994.

Index